KU-765-190

How to Sell with NLP

Books that make you better

Books that make you better. That make you *be* better, *do* better, *feel* better. Whether you want to upgrade your personal skills or change your job, whether you want to improve your managerial style, become a more powerful communicator, or be stimulated and inspired as you work.

Prentice Hall Business is leading the field with a new breed of skills, careers and development books. Books that are a cut above the mainstream – in topic, content and delivery – with an edge and verve that will make you better, with less effort.

Books that are as sharp and smart as you are.

Prentice Hall Business.
We work harder – so you don't have to.

For more details on products, and to contact us, visit
www.pearsoned.co.uk

How to Sell with NLP

The powerful way to guarantee your sales success

Pat Hutchinson

**Prentice Hall
Business**
is an imprint of

Harlow, England • London • New York • Boston • San Francisco • Toronto • Sydney • Singapore • Hong Kong
Tokyo • Seoul • Taipei • New Delhi • Cape Town • Madrid • Mexico City • Amsterdam • Munich • Paris • Milan

PEARSON EDUCATION LIMITED

Edinburgh Gate
Harlow CM20 2JE
Tel: +44 (0)1279 623623
Fax: +44 (0)1279 431059
Website: www.pearsoned.co.uk

First published in Great Britain in 2010

© Pearson Education 2010

The right of Pat Hutchinson to be identified as author of this work has been asserted by her in accordance with the Copyright, Designs and Patents Act 1988.

Pearson Education is not responsible for the content of third party internet sites.

ISBN: 978-0-273-73542-7

British Library Cataloguing-in-Publication Data
A catalogue record for this book is available from the British Library

Library of Congress Cataloging-in-Publication Data
Hutchinson, Pat.
  How to sell with NLP : the powerful way to guarantee your sales success / Pat Hutchinson.
     p. cm.
  Includes index.
  ISBN 978-0-273-73542-7 (pbk.)
  1. Selling. 2. Neurolinguistic programming. 3. Success in business. I. Title.
  HF5438.25.H8677 2010
  658.8501'9--dc22
                              2010022300

All rights reserved. No part of this publication may be reproduced, stored in a retrieval system, or transmitted in any form or by any means, electronic, mechanical, photocopying, recording or otherwise, without either the prior written permission of the publisher or a licence permitting restricted copying in the United Kingdom issued by the Copyright Licensing Agency Ltd, Saffron House, 6–10 Kirby Street, London EC1N 8TS. This book may not be lent, resold, hired out or otherwise disposed of by way of trade in any form of binding or cover other than that in which it is published, without the prior consent of the publisher.

10 9 8 7 6 5 4 3 2 1
14 13 12 11 10

Typeset in 10pt Iowan Old Style BT by 3
Printed and bound in Great Britain by Henry Ling Ltd, Dorchester, Dorset

Contents

About the author

Pat Hutchinson has been extremely fortunate to have pursued both a successful sales career and a career as an NLP trainer. Currently Co-Director of Quadrant 1 International, she has overall responsibility for the sales and marketing function as well as being a lead NLP trainer.

In the early 1990s she rapidly became a top sales executive for a direct selling company – a role that required her not only to sell the company's products but also to build sales teams across the world. Consequently she travelled widely selling and training – often through an interpreter – in the USA, Europe and North Africa and also headed up teams in Japan and Australia. She was consistently listed among the company's highest sales achievers. Pat attributes her success to a cumulative interest in the power of Neuro Linguistic Programming. Eventually becoming a qualified NLP trainer, she made the transition from sales to training and continues to use her sales skills at Quadrant 1 International.

Quadrant 1 International offers a range of NLP-based business programmes covering personal effectiveness, presentation skills and, of course, sales, as well as business-based NLP practitioner and master practitioner programmes (for more about Quadrant 1 International, visit www.quadrant1.com). Here Pat coaches and trains people in organisations in the art and science of using NLP in business.

Pat is the co-author with David Molden of *Brilliant NLP* and *How to be Confident Using the Power of NLP*, both published by Pearson Education.

Acknowledgements

First and foremost thanks go to the originators of NLP – John Grinder and Richard Bandler, without whom many professional people would have been denied the opportunity to supercharge their skills with NLP. Thanks also to the early developers of NLP, including Robert Dilts who gave us the logical levels model – a model that I find is the subject of much creativity among NLP students; to the people who have continually added to the expansive nature of NLP; and to my inspirational teachers along the way – Liz Burns, Ian Newton, Serge Kahali King, Patrick Holford, Lisanne Davidson, Mariella de Martini, Stephen Gilligan and Charles Faulkner.

Very special thanks to my mentor, friend and business partner David Molden, who believed in me, encouraged me and demonstrated unyielding patience on my NLP journey – your support and friendship have been invaluable.

To all the people mentioned in this book whose names have been changed, who added to my learning and who have given me such inspiration as well as rich material to work with: you are all unique – thank you.

Last but not least, thanks to my husband David Hutchinson, for his unwavering love, patience and support.

Introduction: Think, act and sell!

The discovery of DNA has led to the solving of crime in a way that was not possible years ago. Crimes going back many years are now being solved as criminology experts match DNA to items of clothing, furniture and anything else that may have been at the scene of a crime. In the same way, it can be said that the work done by Richard Bandler and John Grinder in the early 1970s, which became known as Neuro Linguistic Programming (NLP), paved the way for people to take more control of their lives by increasing their awareness of the human communication process. Today, NLP is in use in all walks of life as people realise the possibilities of making rapid progress by creating positive change. It is being applied in education, healthcare, sports and business to improve relationships, to influence, to make effective decisions, to motivate and to engage.

In the business arena sales people across a wide range of industries were among the first to embrace NLP skills. Companies, recognising the increased level of sophistication needed to satisfy customers who are no longer taken in by pressurised, hard selling techniques, have been successfully embracing NLP for some time now. Here are just a few areas of sales that are benefiting from the practical application of NLP skills:

- **Consultancy.** Successful consultancy depends on your ability to build relationships, offer alternative solutions and think on the spot. It requires open-mindedness, patience and the ability to assimilate information, as well as the ability to write sometimes complex proposals.

- **Internet selling.** The understanding of human thinking and behaviour offered by NLP will help give your web customers a great user experience. Marketing professionals everywhere are using NLP language skills to write powerful and effective marketing material.

■ **Retail selling.** Achieving sales depend on your ability to be friendly and helpful, to have the language skills to establish exactly what the customer requires and to be able to negotiate honestly and effectively. NLP skills will give you the opportunity to achieve 'add on' sales confidently and effectively.

■ **Party planning/network marketing.** These require the ability to sell products as well as concepts. To sell to small groups of friends and colleagues you need delicacy and tact. Sales need to be fun and entertaining and you will need to be able to 'sell' the idea of a business opportunity to people who may not be aware of the benefits available to them.

■ **Mail order.** This relies on the ability of the marketing department to design an appealing catalogue and of the sales team to 'sell' the catalogue even if it is free.

■ **New ideas and concepts selling.** When Bobby and Sahar Hashemi first established Coffee Republic in the UK they had to convince customers they needed cappuccino-style coffee. Such powers of persuasion now means there are coffee shops on almost every street in every town in the UK, as well as in other parts of the world.

■ **Service selling.** Training falls into this category – where there is nothing tangible to see but instead there is a service promising results. Trusting relationships here are crucial to success.

■ **Non-profit-making sales.** Gaining sponsorship and fund-raising require the ability to build rapport with people who can support your cause.

■ **Selling yourself.** Being able to promote yourself is a skill you will need at some stage in your career. NLP can help you increase your chances of success at every stage of the process – writing your CV, conducting yourself at the interview and delivering a convincing presentation.

Developing business relationships does not stop with the client, prospect or employer. If you are to succeed in your sales role, you will need to spend time building relationships with colleagues in the marketing, finance, logistics and production areas, as well as colleagues in the sales team of your organisation.

This book will teach you awareness skills and techniques to help you expand your sphere of influence with a much wider range of people. It will help you examine your own thinking and behaviour patterns, identify what holds you back and will offer techniques and skills for making changes. It will help you build the confidence and skill level to achieve the levels of success you have always dreamed of. We know this, because many sales professionals who have used these techniques have doubled or trebled their sales as a result – some winning business deals worth in excess of millions of pounds.

Take time to practise what is written here and you will soon find your sales soaring way above their current level, and with the strength and support of your organisation behind you.

The book is designed so that you can either follow it step by step as you progress through the chapters, or dip in and out of it as and when you please. The examples used are all real (with the names changed), and I have deliberately picked examples from all types of industries and sales environments. The tools and techniques explained here are universal and so I encourage you to enjoy experimenting with them wherever you find yourself.

Whatever stage your selling career has reached, I know you will find something here to explore and to pass on to your teams. Enjoy making it easy for people to buy from you!

01

Selling in the twenty-first century

The world of sales is changing. Far from having an adverse effect on business relationships, technology and the advent of social networking is having a positive and vibrant impact, particularly in the world of sales. Business relationships are now carried out in the public eye all over the world via such networks as LinkedIn, Facebook and Plaxo. Relationships are becoming more visible, and recommendations about the quality of work you can offer are available for all to see at the click of a button. In the same way that websites became the face of your business a few years ago, networking sites are now the new face of you. In his excellent book *Blind Faith*, Ben Elton gives a tongue-in-cheek portrayal of a futuristic society where nothing is sacred any more – we can have anything we like streamed into our living rooms, even to the point where we can judge Joe next door's performance in the bedroom! Let's hope that a modicum of decorum prevails before we get to that stage, but let's also celebrate the positive impact such technology is having.

So what does this have to do with sales?

A changing landscape

The advent of voicemail has made it easy to filter calls, and often it's the sales call that gets filtered during busy times. Cold calling is being replaced by a number of alternative customer-attracting initiatives, such as e-mail marketing, advertising on high-usage social networking and popular websites, introductions through networking sites, and in some cases a return to traditional ways of advertising through direct mail. All these developments create both challenges and opportunities for marketing teams eager to get their brands in front of their markets, as well as for sales teams learning how to build relationships and win clients in this constantly evolving buyer/seller online landscape.

Building social networks online means there is no hiding place. People all over the world can read your profile, your background, where you went to school, who you are friends with and what you do in your spare time. Will this ever replace the Sunday morning round of golf, Saturday afternoon at a football match or a night in a wine bar? Probably not, but social networking is allowing us to reach far greater numbers of people in an instant. We need to know how best to utilise these networks, which are sprouting up everywhere. The key is to build long-term, robust relationships that focus on mutual benefits and can stand the test of public scrutiny as well as time. With key influencers moving freely from one organisation to another, a strong, well-built relationship can carry you a long way in your sales and business career.

How we buy

Being able to buy online has also changed the role of the sales person. Perhaps paradoxically it has radically increased the need to understand human behaviour and buying patterns. How do we search on the internet, how long will we stay on a site and what attracts us about the site? Is it the words, is it the pictures or is it the tone of the site?

All these changes have made the need for advanced communication skills even greater, and you will find the tools and techniques in this book just as applicable to selling via a website, e-mail and the telephone as they are to more traditional one-to-one and group scenarios.

The sales person as facilitator

Bearing in mind the increasing need to build long-lasting, robust and trusting relationships with your prospects and clients, I will be focusing on how we, as sales people, view these buyers. Many sales training books set out well-planned strategies for 'baiting' their prey or use warlike metaphors for the sales process, suggesting that one side is going to 'win' over the other. These books ask you to behave like a coiled cobra waiting to pounce and talk about half-nelson closes. I am sure there is not a person on this planet who would like to think that you are thinking like this during a sales process. This type of thinking is no longer appropriate if we are going to build the type of relationships that will endure over long periods of time and stand up to public scrutiny. Buyers are more sophisticated and aware today than ever before and are not fooled by gimmicks and insincerity in pursuit of a sale. I prefer to think of the role of a sales person as a facilitator whose job it is to help the buyer to make informed and profitable decisions about the product or service on offer. In other words, your role as a sales person is to use your skills to make it easy for customers to buy from you. This way, everyone wins: there are no preconceived barriers to the process and your integrity remains intact throughout.

Everyone is in sales

As an employee or representative of your organisation, you never know when you will be called upon to 'sell'.

Whether you call it 'sales' or not, everyone is a sales person. If you are being interviewed for a job, you are technically selling yourself. There is no such thing as a job for life any more, so there is a need to sell your experience, skills and attitude on an increasingly regular basis. If you have an idea, you will want to sell it to the powers that be in order to get it off the ground. Similarly, if you see someone you would like to have a relationship with, then you are going to make out a good case for them to reciprocate.

So what is NLP?

Quite simply put, Neuro Linguistic Programming (NLP) describes the way we use our brain and nervous system to communicate our thoughts and feelings using verbal and non-verbal language. Most of the time our communication follows set habits or programmes. These programmes are created unconsciously by any number of both positive and negative experiences from outside sources, including family, friends, television, teachers, books, colleagues and managers. Some programmes work well and get great results. Others act as barriers, hindering progress and achievement. This is as true for sales as it is for any other endeavour. NLP gives you the tools to consciously take control of your programming and make it work more productively.

NLP is built on a number of presuppositions, or beliefs as they are more commonly known. I will introduce these as they become appropriate throughout the book. The first one to consider is:

The person with the most flexibility is in control.

It stands to reason that a person with only one type of response or behaviour in any given situation is going to get only one type of result. NLP teaches us to flex our behaviour to get different, more productive results if something isn't working. For example, if you have made up your mind that all sales proposals should be long and detailed, then you are only going to appeal to those prospects who share your value on detail and who have the time to read your proposals. If, on the other hand, you take the trouble to ask your client how they would like to see the proposal presented, then you will widen your prospects list to include those who simply want a one- or two-page outline.

Here is another presupposition of NLP:

If you always do what you have always done, you will always get what you have always had.

In other words, if you want a different result, you need to do something different. This whole book is about increasing your flexibility of behaviour so that you can change it in an instant in order to achieve a different result.

Why NLP and sales?

It is very easy to communicate with people who are like you. It is often said that 'people buy people' and we generally buy from people or organisations we like, trust and understand. This like, trust and understanding is based on some complex, but easy to comprehend, unconscious structures. By understanding and utilising these structures, you can communicate persuasively with a wider range of people, including those who are unlike you and those you have found puzzling. NLP gives you the tools and techniques to pick up and tune into buying patterns and to interact with prospects in a way that is most persuasive.

Example

A friend of mine recently moved house. She confided that her decision for choosing a removal firm was made on the basis of the person who arrived to assess the job. By the time he left the house she had decided that he was the man for the job, even before she received the quote, which was by no means the cheapest. It transpired later that this man had retired from his corporate role to set up his own removal business. He had become an NLP practitioner years earlier and knew very well how to build business relationships that resulted in lucrative sales.

Successful sales people:

- know that everyone is in sales;

- recognise that the world of sales is changing, due to technology and social networking;

- recognise that NLP will help them to sell to a much wider range of people;

- build strong, mutually beneficial relationships and facilitate the sales process;

- continually practise increasing their behavioural flexibility;

- become more determined with every rejection;

- focus on doing everything they can to make it easy for clients to buy from them.

02

Building strong relationships

In Chapter 1 you learnt how the world of sales is changing, resulting in an even greater need for building strong, trusting business relationships. Such relationships require an awareness of a number of behavioural characteristics demonstrated by you and your clients and prospects. When you learn how these characteristics interplay with each other, you will be able to significantly expand your sphere of influence in your marketplace.

Ben's story

Ben started his career in the IT software industry 15 years ago, full of enthusiasm and raw energy. He attended a sales training programme to learn the finer points of his products and was given a sales process to follow, which included how to qualify his prospects, how to present and how to handle objections. He also received some tips on how to handle the emotional stress of disappointment when prospects just weren't ready to buy. Initially his enthusiasm carried him through and he learnt to bat off the rejections and stay focused on the process. He achieved some excellent results and made up his mind that selling was definitely for him. He settled into the routine of arranging appointments, making presentations and watching his sales grow, and he even won international awards for his efforts.

It was some time before Ben noticed that his sales had levelled off, his colleagues were beginning to overtake him and that he was no longer number one in his company. For a time he pushed this growing realisation to the back of his mind, and then slowly, almost imperceptibly, he began to blame outside factors – the market had changed, there was more competition, the pricing structure was wrong, the product was no longer funky, there was high unemployment in his area. After three years Ben left his job and moved to another company, where he repeated the pattern, but this time he did it consciously – preparing himself for the downfall so that when it came he was already moving out and on to the next role.

Each time he changed jobs, the more energy and enthusiasm he was losing – in fact friends who knew him before he became a sales person hardly recognised him. He was drinking and smoking more, generally not looking after himself, and rarely socialising because he felt lethargic and miserable.

It was easy for Ben to fall into this way of thinking. Although he had received some initial training and some advice on how to deal with the knocks, he had not fully prepared himself for a career in sales. He lacked personal awareness and did not spend enough time focusing on his own personal contribution to the process. He did not see himself like others did, knew nothing about his own thinking and behavioural patterns and consequently did not know how to flex them to match those of his prospects. His early successes were generated from sheer enthusiasm and came from a group of prospects whose natural inclination was to respond to such enthusiasm. When the going got tough – as it inevitably did when the enthusiasm waned – then sales became harder and harder to achieve and Ben did not know how to flex his behaviour to reverse the trend. Gradually he found reasons not to call his contacts and bit by bit his career fell apart.

Changing for the better

What Ben failed to realise is that in order to succeed in a twenty-first-century selling environment things had to change. Here is how:

■ The advent of social networking means that increasingly the emphasis needs to be on building long-term relationships and not just on short- and medium-term sales targets.

■ In a relationship a more holistic approach is needed – you need to have a heightened level of personal awareness to know how you are impacting the relationship and how to alter your approach when appropriate.

▪ Taking responsibility for adding value for customers is a key part of the sales role.

▪ Looking after yourself and staying aligned with what is important to you, your customer and your environment are key features of successful sales people.

Pure enthusiasm, product knowledge and a sales process are a good foundation, but skilful selling requires a lot more. Skilful sales people have an excellent relationship with themselves, with their prospects and clients, and with the activities in which they engage, as well as with their products and services – as shown in Figure 2.1.

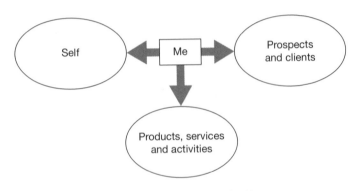

Figure 2.1 Excellent sales people work on all types of relationships

Getting ready to sell by building an excellent relationship with yourself

Most people accept that it is easier to sell to people like themselves than it is to sell to people who are different. Common ground, a similar sense of humour and shared backgrounds all contribute to quick rapport building, opening doors and an opportunity to explore possibilities. But if you restrict your market to just the people with whom you have these things in common, you are greatly limiting your potential. Because relationship building is an unconscious process, you may not be aware of what attracts you to certain people or them to you, or indeed how to go about building the relationship – it is automatic. This chapter therefore has two intentions:

- To give you an understanding of your own thinking and behaviour patterns so that you can flex them when you come into contact with people who don't necessarily share them and who you may find confusing or difficult.

- To understand other people's thinking and behaviour patterns so that you can recognise them and flex your behaviour accordingly.

Carrying out such changes with integrity requires you to consider another presupposition of NLP:

Respect other people's maps of the world.

NLP recognises the uniqueness of every individual on the planet. No two people are absolutely identical in the way they think and behave. Even identical twins display patterns that are unique to each of them. NLP goes even further than this in recognising that not only is everyone different but also people themselves behave differently at different times. NLP is often referred to as the study of subjective experience, i.e. the study of human behaviour as it is happening in the moment. It is useful, therefore, to refrain from making judgements about another person's way of thinking or, as NLP prefers to call it, 'their map of the world'. A person's map consists of a unique blend of values, beliefs, metaprogrammes and experience, all filtered and stored in a way that is personal to each individual. Maintaining respect for people's unique maps and paying attention to the here and now of human behaviour will allow you to do your job with integrity and understanding.

Metaprogrammes

People think and behave differently according to their meta-programme profiles. Metaprogrammes can be described as behaviours that result from some general principles that are important to you. There is no right or wrong to these patterns – just a set of results that occur from applying them, which may be productive in some contexts but not in others. Also, we need to remember that people can behave from a different profile in different contexts. For example, you may feel that timekeeping at work is very important and make sure that you arrive for meetings on time and well prepared. If this is the case, you will probably also make sure that meetings do not overrun and expect others to do the same. Perhaps you even wear a watch at work, which you remove when you arrive home, where time may not be so important to you. Your friends may even have a completely different perception of the importance you place on timekeeping.

Below are some examples of profiles that will have a significant impact on you as a sales person. Remember that your profile will have an effect on your own personal approach to selling. You also need to be aware of these profiles when negotiating with someone who may operate from the opposite pattern. Although these patterns are dealt with individually in the following sections, it is the combination of patterns that will impact the way you respond to different scenarios. I will say more about this at the end of the chapter.

Think of these patterns as a see-saw with maximum flexibility at the balance point in the middle and extreme behaviour at each end. In the following sections I will describe the extreme behaviour of each pattern, how to recognise it in yourself and others and how to use it effectively in the sales process. Where your patterns match, you are likely to be able to build quick rapport – it is where they don't match that you will need to flex your presentation accordingly. To help you remember them, I have given them cartoon names.

Self-assessments

At the beginning of each of the following metaprogramme sections is a brief self-assessment designed to help you assess your own position on the continuum. Completing this before you read on will give you a more accurate idea of your own metaprogramme patterns. Each pair of questions or statements has a total value of 5 and you are asked to divide this value between the two statements as follows:

- If A is completely characteristic of what you would do and B is completely uncharacteristic, score 5 on A and 0 on B.

- If A is almost completely characteristic but you might sometimes favour B, score 4 on A and 1 on B.

- If A is only slightly more characteristic than B, score 3 on A and 2 on B.

- If B is only slightly more characteristic than A, score 3 on B and 2 on A.

- If B is almost completely characteristic but you might sometimes favour A, score 4 on B and 1 on A.

- If B is completely characteristic of what you would do and A is completely uncharacteristic, score 5 on B and 0 on A.

Make sure you answer the questions from the perspective of your sales role, as metaprogrammes can change in different contexts. Keep your answers spontaneous and remember that there are no right or wrong answers – only consequences that may serve you well sometimes and not so well at others.

When you have finished, add up your A scores and your B scores for each group of statements. You will now have a total of 15 divided between A and B, e.g. A=7, B=8 or A=10, B=5. At the end of this chapter there are guidelines on interpreting your scores. Remember this is not a psychometric test – it is to help you flex your behaviour so that you can relate to people who may not share your patterns, and also to help you to recognise the patterns in others.

Towards/away from
Self-assessment

1 I usually get up in the morning to:

A	B

    A   Avoid creating a problem if I don't.

    B   Look forward to the day ahead.

2 When I want to set myself targets to aim for:

A	B

    A   I often find it difficult to decide what to aim for.

    B   I have no trouble in setting targets.

3 In most situations:

A	B

    A   I know what to avoid or what I do not want to happen.

    B   I often find it difficult to know what I should avoid.

Total

A	B

Now read on for more information about these patterns.

Tina Towards and Aristotle Away From

Tina Towards gets up in the morning thinking about the targets, goals and plans for the day and is excited about the prospects of new ideas and challenges. She is unlikely to be phased by limitations and focuses on the end result. When things don't go to plan, she will move quickly on to the next challenge without always assessing what may have gone wrong.

Tina gets on well with forward-thinking and open-minded prospects because they respect her approach to challenges. They listen to ideas that are likely to add value to their business and share her dislike of risk aversion. They use words and phrases such as visionary, future, goals, targets, bottom line, moving forward, looking to the future, forecasting and envisaging, and are unlikely to use words such as safety, security, protection, risk and insurance. Together they appear to be a dynamic duo.

Tina knows instinctively that by asking these prospects such questions as 'If you were to buy our product/service today, what would you want it to do for your organisation?' they will answer in forward-thinking, positive terms and probably be able to envisage and describe the products in use.

Tina likes serving her towards-focused clients, and ends her day feeling vibrant and exhilarated, so much so that she actively plans her day to ensure that she includes more and more of these types of people, gradually pushing the ones she does not understand to the bottom of her action list.

When eventually she has to pay Aristotle Away From a visit, Tina ends the meeting feeling exhausted and despondent. Every time she asks him a towards-based question (for example, 'How do you see your company using this product?'), he tells her that he is worried about how the change might affect the people in accounts, or how much time will be involved in the change-over or how costly the product is. His away-from approach is based around security, a concept that Tina finds difficult to understand. He uses words and phrases such as safety, fear, security, protection and risk, and begins sentences with 'I don't want ...'. Tina fails to make an impression with her forward-thinking approach and leaves the meeting feeling frustrated, writing him off or at the very least vowing not to visit again for a long, long time.

What can they do?

If Tina changed her approach very slightly she could begin to make an impact on Aristotle. Aristotle's main motivation is security. She needs to reassure him that everything will be OK, dealing with his worries and encouraging him to take a step forward by including some of the consequences of not taking action. Aristotle's motivation is to avoid pain – for example, to avoid failure, to avoid the embarrassment of the competition getting ahead, to ensure that bad things don't happen – and he will take action to avoid these things happening. Tina must use the utmost integrity and be clear in her belief that the product is right for the organisation. Aristotle requires a lot of reassurance and is unlikely to respond to what he perceives as her naturally 'gung-ho' approach.

Organisations can become stuck at the extremes of these two patterns. Being entirely towards as an organisation can bring success and develop a positive culture that encourages creativity. It attracts people who like a challenge and who aren't afraid to test out new ideas. Job security is not something they generally concern themselves with; they celebrate their success and exude an air of confidence. Sometimes success and celebration can be so much part of the culture that it becomes the norm and it may take such a company a while to notice when things are not going to plan.

People who are motivated by security are not generally attracted to such organisations. They are more likely to work in places where the perks are good and perceived job security is a given. These organisations include risk management, insurance companies and the public sector.

Example

Sally is a jewellery sales person. She took an order for six medium-sized cubic zirconia bracelets for her client. When the delivery arrived Sally realised that she had been sent six large bracelets. Her towards-thinking pattern enabled her to increase her sales for that month. Instead of complaining about the delivery and returning the order to the warehouse, she reordered the medium bracelets and found six new customers for the larger ones.

If, like Aristotle, you have a strong away-from motivation you are likely to continue with your role because of what may happen if you don't – you'll miss your targets, lose your job, won't be able to feed the family and so on. You would avoid difficult clients and situations if you could but you will probably persevere out of concern for what might happen if you don't. This may be good for your organisation but makes life tough for you. Try making life easier by consciously focusing on the positive aspects of your role, the people you come into contact with and the results you achieve.

Certain industries attract people who have away-from patterns – for example, the insurance industry services people who favour security and take out lots of insurance policies 'just in case'. The corner shop that opens at all hours serves a community of people who like the security of knowing that they can pick up the things they have forgotten at the supermarket or may need late at night.

Buying motivations

- **Towards**: I'll buy it because it will make us more competitive/efficient/productive.
- **Away from**: I'll buy it because I'm concerned about what might happen if I don't and it will make us safer/more secure/less likely to get caught out.

Options/procedures

Self-assessment

1 I find it motivational to:

    A   Do the things I really must do.

    B   Explore opportunities and possibilities.

A	B

2 When the chips are down I have a tendency to:

    A   Carry on regardless.

    B   Look for other options.

A	B

3 When I get involved in my work:

    A   I would prefer to work to a set plan of action.

    B   I enjoy considering new alternatives.

Total

A	B

Now read on for more information about these patterns.

Olivia Options and Peter Procedures

Olivia Options loves to have choice in her life. She likes the idea that her sales role gives her a wide range of industry types to cover, a range of functions within those industries and a product range that offers her lots of choice. Her open, expressive body language makes her easily identifiable and the use of words such as choices, options, alternatives, possibilities and ideas gives her pattern away. Her biggest challenge is where to start, because having made a decision then her choice is removed, but while the choice remains then she feels good. This is a bit like buyer's remorse. While the choice is available Olivia can ponder the options happily, but as soon as she has made a decision about something she wonders what it would have been like to have chosen a different path.

The same may apply in her social life – lots of restaurants to choose from, lots of shops to visit, lots of physical activities to get involved in and lots of different things to do on the same evening. Sometimes Olivia ends up doing nothing in the evenings simply because making the choice is too stressful. As a sales person she may appear scatty as she can change her mind at a moment's notice and does not appear to have a set procedure for approaching her work. She often leaves her customers confused because she offers them so many alternatives that they are unclear as to the best course of action. She then wonders why she has difficulty completing a sale and blames her customers for being indecisive.

Peter Procedures, on the other hand, has a very structured approach to his work. His habit of emphasising his points on his fingers or using his hands to suggest a linear process indicate his procedural approach. He makes lists and uses words and phrases such as step by step, firstly, next, procedure, point 1, point 2, point 3, need to, have to and must. He has a system that he follows rigidly, knows exactly how many calls he needs to make to get a result and returns home satisfied that he has followed the procedure, irrespective of whether or not his day has been successful in terms of sales. But his need to follow procedures often causes him to miss key signals, for example that the prospect is or is not ready to move on, or wants to miss a step and get to the agreement signing. He can also become flummoxed in sales meetings if his prospects ask for alternatives to his suggestions or call him to change arrangements at the last minute. On such occasions he may accuse his customers of being disorganised or even disrespectful, and he may find himself gravitating towards those that are like him – organised and structured – while unconsciously avoiding those who cause disruption to his procedural approach.

What can they do?

Heightened awareness is the answer here. Peter needs to learn to be more flexible with his clients, offering them enough alternative solutions to their buying challenges to allow them to make a decision without confusion. His procedures can incorporate a process for generating such options. In the same way, he can reduce his frustration if he develops a procedure for dealing with last-minute changes.

Olivia, on the other hand, can help herself by taking a leaf out of Peter's book. One way to do this is by a process of elimination: looking at the choices that really do not provide the best solution and honing them down to a manageable number. To succeed with clients who share Peter's pattern, she will need to take them through the entire sales process step by step, telling them what time she will arrive, what to expect from the meeting and what she expects to happen during and after the meeting. This way, they know exactly where they are and what will take place and they feel comfortable.

Example

Tim is a search engine optimisation sales person. His approach is to identify an industry sector and work his way through a list of companies who match the criteria within the particular industry he selects. The process often takes a number of telephone calls while his prospects compare his offering with that of other companies. During every telephone call Tim repeats the list of benefits his company has to offer as part of his procedure. His prospects often find this irritating as it interrupts the flow of natural conversation, but he seems unaware of this and ploughs on in the same way regardless.

Tim has adopted a procedural approach to his selling and becomes confused when potential customers deviate from his procedure. The perception of his clients can often be that he is not listening and that he is pushy and inflexible.

Buying motivations

- **Options**: I can't decide which one to have so I will either procrastinate or buy it in all three colours and specifications.

- **Procedures**: This is a repeat order or someone else has said they need it [a direction].

Through time/in time

Self-assessment

1 If you were to arrive 15 minutes late to a sales meeting, how would you act?

A	B

  A   Be tough on yourself for not being punctual.

  B   Apologise and forget it.

2 Which of the following describes your general behaviour?

A	B

  A   Always on time for appointments, often arriving with time to spare.

  B   Often rushing from A to B to avoid being late.

3 I tend to work mostly:

A	B

  A   To a predefined and set plan.

  B   By responding to situations as they arise.

Total

A	B

Now read on for more information about these patterns.

Thelma Through Time and Ian In Time

Thelma Through Time values her time and expects others to do the same. She plans her working schedule in fine detail and ensures that she always arrives at appointments in good time. She has an innate sense of how long it takes to do things – to prepare, travel, conduct a meeting and move on to the next one. If something happens to upset her planning, Thelma may become agitated. If she is unavoidably late for an appointment, she can be thrown into confusion and may mentally chide herself for not having organised things better. If people keep her waiting beyond the scheduled time to meet, she can feel undervalued and may begin to fret about getting to her next appointment. She sometimes appears to value the schedule itself more than she does the intended outcome.

Example

Chris is a software sales person. He is meticulous about his schedule and hates being late for anything. He once booked an appointment with a prospect in the centre of a busy market town. As he arrived at the outskirts of the town, he realised there was a festival taking place and heavy traffic was causing major hold-ups. Chris knew he was going to be late. Instead of calling his prospect to apologise, he turned around, returned home and asked one of his colleagues to call the prospect saying that he had been taken ill. He couldn't bear the thought of being late and equally didn't want his client to think he was a poor timekeeper – such was the value he placed on being on time.

Ian In Time, on the other hand, may plan with the best of intentions but his ability to place strong importance on what is happening at this moment in time means that he can be easily distracted. When you are with him, Ian makes you feel valued as he gives you his full attention, not worrying about what he has to do next. However, when you are not around then something or someone else will capture his attention and he will become absorbed in what has now become the present moment for him. His concept of time can get him into trouble as his schedule starts to slip and his day gets longer and longer. His through-time clients may find him frustrating as he is invariably late for appointments, offering only a cursory apology, which to the through-timer may appear insincere. He often runs out of time during meetings and may not leave enough time to sum up and complete the sale.

What can they do?

Thelma can help herself by changing the way she judges people who don't share her concept of time. Believing that they disrespect her causes her to feel bad towards these people, complain about them and conclude that they are not interested in her products. They then find their way to the bottom of her priority list. Understanding that in-time people place their importance on the present moment will help her to realise that once she does manage to get in front of these people she will have their full attention.

Ian, on the other hand, needs to be aware that through-time people are judging him and his inability to keep to time. They may use words such as disorganised and inconsiderate, and disregard his project range as a consequence. Planning more carefully, giving advance warning if he is running late and apologising sincerely when he is will all help with his customer relationships.

Buying motivations

■ **Through time**: I'll see if I can plan it into next year's budget.

■ **In time**: I'll have it now! What do you mean you can't deliver it for three months?

Considering/doing

Self-assessment

1 I am good at:

    A   Getting the job done.

    B   Analysing and understanding the situation.

A	B

2 Which set of words would you tend to use?

    A   Go for it, just do it, why wait, right now.

    B   Give it some thought, consider this, understand, look before you leap.

A	B

3 I would rather be:

    A   An entrepreneur.

    B   A researcher.

A	B

Total

A	B

Now read on for more information about these patterns.

Carrie Considering and Donny Doing

Carrie Considering spends a lot of time getting ready to sell. She is likely to research her clients well, consider the market and think carefully about which products are most suited to which prospect or client. When meeting with clients, she will ask them to consider the implications of buying her products or services and give them plenty of time to do so. She often runs into difficulties when clients 'go cold' because she has not taken control of the sale early enough. She may also have problems completing the sale, missing the buying signal from the client as she considers too long.

Donny Doing, on the other hand, can't wait to get going. He is keen to get to his prospects and is often in his car and on the road long before Carrie leaves her desk. He appears as 'action man' to his clients, although sometimes he can come unstuck through lack of preparation. People who like to consider frustrate him and he often avoids communicating with them because of his high need for action. He often describes them as indecisive and unable to make a decision.

Example

Darren was considering expanding his pure water company into Asian markets. He ran the idea past his colleagues, friends, bank manager and some customers with an interest in the markets. He drew up a viable business plan and created a strategy for the expansion. However, he still did not feel ready and delayed his starting date for, what appeared to others around him, no apparent reason. Darren himself did not feel he had considered all the possible angles and wanted to further his research. In the meantime his biggest competitor had picked up on his idea and was already making waves in the markets.

What can they do?

Carrie would improve her performance if she evolved a set of criteria that represented an appropriate amount of considering and disciplined herself to stick to it. For example, she could design a simple checklist of things to consider with a limit on the amount of information under each heading. By taking a leaf out of Donny's book, i.e. focusing on taking action, she could also learn to complete her sales sooner rather than later.

Donny may scare off those clients who prefer to take their time and consider the implications of buying before making a decision. He can prevent them from dropping to the bottom of his priority list by simply building in a little time for them to reflect before asking for the sale.

Buying motivations

■ **Considering**: I'd like to talk to my colleagues, check the figures, match the colours, do some market research and test the durability.

■ **Doing**: Let's get on with it. What do you want me to do next? Where do I sign?

Internal reference/external reference
Self-assessment

1 If someone tries to tell me what they think I should do:

A	B

A   I would resist and use my own judgement.

B   I would welcome their opinions and take their ideas into full consideration.

2 When I have completed a task successfully:

A	B

A   I don't need anyone else to tell me I have done it well.

B   I really appreciate someone else telling me that the task was done well.

3 If I have to make an important decision, I would prefer to:

A	B

A   Work it out for myself without outside interference.

B   Find out the best course of action by asking other people what I should do.

Total

A	B

Now read on for more information about these patterns.

Ingrid Internal Reference and Eric External Reference

Ingrid Internal Reference does not need other people to tell her when she is succeeding. She has an inbuilt sense of when something has gone well and consequently does not necessarily ask the client for their feedback or viewpoint. If by any chance a client proffers an opposing viewpoint, Ingrid may take the view that they do not know what they are talking about and mentally write them off as a potential client. When people ask her for her opinion she gives it freely, but may form a mental judgement about her questioner's perceived lack of personal opinion. She can also sometimes appear arrogant and opinionated to her clients.

Eric External Reference values the opinions of others and is constantly asking his clients, his colleagues and his friends and family for feedback. He takes this on board readily and adjusts his behaviour accordingly. He can come unstuck in the boardroom because many senior executives are internally referenced and can perceive his constant pursuit of feedback as displaying a lack of security or self-esteem. They may refer to him as 'unsure of himself' and therefore unsure of his products. Eric often feels that he has not been able to sell his products effectively and sometimes does not understand why people are not convinced by him.

What can they do?

Ingrid needs to be aware that other people might just have a different opinion, which she needs to explore if she is to succeed. Making a point of asking for an opinion and then listening to the response, with the intention to understand rather than paying cursory acknowledgement, is a skill she needs to develop.

Eric can make a small change to his approach when dealing with internally referenced clients: instead of asking 'What do you think?' of his clients, he can turn his question into a statement beginning with 'And, of course, you know that ...'. Unconsciously the internally referenced client is saying, 'Yes, of course I know.'

Buying motivations

- **Internal reference**: I know this is the right thing to do.
- **External reference**: I'll buy it because the team/you/my family/ friends think it's a good idea [will probably ask for feedback from interested parties first].

Global/detail

Self-assessment

1 When given a big task to do, I would much prefer to:

A	B

  A Break it down into smaller, more manageable tasks.

  B Concentrate on the overall direction of the task.

2 If interrupted when explaining something to another person, I would prefer to:

A	B

  A Go back to the beginning and start again.

  B Start from where I left off and move forward.

3 When asked to decide how to do something, I would prefer to start by:

  A Establishing all the facts I need to know before making any decisions.

  B Looking at the 'big picture' first to help me put the facts in the proper places.

Now read on for more information about these patterns.

Gloria Global and Destiny Detail

Gloria Global has a high-level view of what a successful sale looks like. She likes to talk big-picture and strategic ideas to her clients and may not be able to answer detailed questions when asked. She often appears lacking in knowledge to her more detail-oriented clients and they may describe her as 'airy fairy' or vague. Gloria gets on well in boardrooms where directors often only want to know, 'Does it work, how much and when can we have it?' She can often complete sales quickly but may fail to follow through effectively, disliking the need for detailed preparation of proposals, quotes, orders and delivery arrangements.

Destiny Detail loves to regale her clients with her knowledge of her products and takes great care to make sure they are subjected to every last one of them. She can easily fill the allotted time for a sales presentation with this, details about her day, how she arrived at the meeting and the intricacies of the new CRM system her company has adopted, leaving little time to assess the client needs and finalise the sale. Her clients and prospects often make excuses when she tries to book appointments with them, since they do not feel able to give her the amount of time she appears to require to make a sale. She gets frustrated at her inability to build relationships with her prospects, who often describe her as tedious.

What can they do?

Gloria needs to learn to ask whether her prospects have enough information to make a decision and be prepared to provide exactly what it is they are asking for. Her big-picture approach means that she will often leave out important facts and arrangements. A checklist will help here.

Destiny needs to discipline herself to draw back from the detail and focus on the overall sale. She can do this by deciding beforehand the key facts about her products that are going to help her clients solve their issues, and by making a concerted effort not to answer cursory questions at great length.

Buying motivations

- **Global**: I like the idea, someone else can sort out the details.
- **Detail**: I'll buy when I have all the information I need [make sure your proposal covers everything].

Sameness/difference

Self-assessment

1 When I have choice over the type of work I do, I prefer:

A	B

   A Tasks that are similar to what I have done before.

   B Tasks that are completely new to me.

2 If you were to take a job with a different company, which would you enjoy the most?

A	B

   A A company with well-established processes and methods.

   B A company where the requirements and methods are frequently changing.

3 Which set of words has the most appeal for you?

A	B

   A Consistent, alike, identical, standard, adjacent.

   B Unique, changing, new, different, opposite.

A	B

Now read on for more information about these patterns.

Sammy Sameness and Diana Difference

Sammy Sameness looks for things to remain the same. When comparing, for example, two occasions, products, scenarios, people, companies or processes against each other, he will always look for similarities between the two. He is at his most comfortable when he recognises situations and people and can repeat his sales process almost to the letter. At home he may follow a similar pattern – still in touch with old friends from school, living in the same area or even the same house as he has done for many years, holidaying in the same place and taking the same route to work every day. His client list consists of people he knows well.

Diana Difference, on the other hand, cannot bear repetition. Her boredom threshold is low and she often changes jobs in the quest for something different. In her personal life she often moves house, is always decorating and moves around from one group of friends to another. She rarely gets to know her clients well as she is on to her next job before this can happen.

What can they do?

Sammy will limit his client base if he does not spread his wings and look further than his own backyard. Chances are that he is happy with the solid customer base he has built up over the years and the routine he has developed to serve them, but in this age of constant change he needs to extend his area of influence.

Diana, in contrast, needs to satisfy her difference pattern from within her role, or otherwise she will always be moving on and never achieve excellence. She needs to consider how she can introduce variety – within the role, through her customers, through her product range or in her area of responsibility.

Buying motivations

■ **Sameness**: Excellent, we won't have to make too many changes: this product means we can continue the way we have been.

■ **Difference**: That's great: it's new and it's different – bring it on.

Independent/co-operative
Self-assessment

1 When I feel it is time to recharge my batteries, I prefer to be:

A	B

A Alone.

B With people.

2 When I am working on a project, I am more effective if I:

A	B

A Have sole responsibility for the project.

B Share responsibility with others.

3 If I am working on my own in an office, I concentrate better by:

A	B

A Keeping the door closed to avoid distractions.

B Allowing occasional interruptions to give me a break and help me refocus.

Total

A	B

Now read on for more information about these patterns.

Irene Independent and Carmen Co-operative

Irene Independent loves working on her own. She chose her sales role because she knew that she would be totally responsible for reaching her own targets, could work from home, plan her own schedule and not be distracted by all the activity at head office. On the occasions when she has to visit head office for a meeting, she often attends the meeting and then sneaks away to an office on her own where she can work quietly, catching up on e-mails and making phone calls.

Carmen Co-operative, unlike Irene, loves the buzz of the office and finds it very uncomfortable working on her own. She will happily work away in her open-plan office, contributing to the banter every now and again, catching up on the social side of activities and absorbing any new company information she may need by just being around.

What can they do?

Both Carmen and Irene selected sales roles that would suit their personal preference in relation to this metaprogramme. Both would find it awkward working in the other's environment.

Changing this preference is not going to add or subtract greatly to Irene or Carmen's ability to sell. Irene may sometimes find herself missing things in the office and Carmen may find herself easily distracted, but on the whole their results will not be hindered by this pattern unless they are forced to work in an environment that does not suit their personal preference.

Buying motivations

- **Independent**: This will help everyone to be more independent.
- **Co-operative**: This will be great for team-working/the family/ friends.

It's the whole profile that counts

Combinations of these patterns can either balance or enhance extreme behaviours. For example, a combination of <u>away-from</u> and <u>external-reference</u> patterns may cause someone to seek out negative evidence from other people to support their thinking. Unfortunately, with this combination positive feedback can be disregarded and the person often gives themselves a hard time, mentally beating themselves up for not performing well.

A combination of <u>considering and options</u> patterns is a recipe for procrastination, as this person has to perform the considering process with all the options. <u>Options and doing</u>, on the other hand, can balance each other out – this person will only be able to tolerate choice for as long as they can resist taking action.

<u>Sameness and procedures</u> is a recipe for inflexibility. Lacking the creativity to be able to generate options, this person will happily continue with existing procedures, feeling comfortable doing so as a result of the sameness pattern. <u>Difference and options</u>, on the other hand, is a recipe for inconsistency, as this person may get bored easily and want to try a number of different options.

Noticing these patterns both in yourself and in your prospective clients will help you to adjust your sales approach. It will also help you to remain curious about people so that you refrain from making judgements that may affect your ability to sell to people you find puzzling or different from you.

Assessment scores

Now that you have totalled your scores, take a look at the ones where you score 10 or more. These are the ones you need to be aware of and to work on – anything less than 10 indicates that you have flexibility between the two extremes of the continuum. For example, 9 on options and 6 on procedures means that you can be flexible between these two behaviours.

Learn to be curious, refrain from being judgemental

At the beginning of this chapter I stressed the importance of respecting other people's maps of the world. This takes self-control and practice as you learn to develop more curiosity to replace judgement. It is human nature to make judgements and to put meanings to the things that happen around us. We grow up asking the question 'Why?' and develop a need to find reasons for the way people behave. The faster we live our lives, the faster we can find meanings:

- He didn't look at the brochure [means that] he can't have been interested.
- He probably won't buy [because] he cancelled the meeting.
- They cancelled the last contract [means that] we must be too expensive.
- These people are tough cookies [which means that] I'll never be able to sell anything to them.
- He hasn't answered my e-mail [means that] he is far too busy to speak to me.

Placing a negative meaning and therefore judging a situation in this way is to limit potential. Negative thinking results in negative behaviour and the chances are that none of the above thinking patterns will result in a sale. Being curious, on the other hand, will allow you to remain open-minded and to pursue a different approach:

- He didn't look at the brochure – maybe he didn't have time on this occasion or maybe he has already researched the products on the internet. Perhaps he prefers to listen to a description of them or see them in action.

- He cancelled the meeting – I am sure he had his reasons, which he will tell me later. Maybe he hasn't had time to speak to the stakeholders, maybe something happened at home – I know him well enough to ask.

- They cancelled the contract – I am curious to find out what caused them to do that. I'll give them a call tomorrow.

- These people are good at their jobs and I know they will respect the fact that I am good at mine. Preparing for this meeting will be an exciting challenge.

- He didn't answer my e-mail – I will try to catch up with him again when he has more time.

Each of these responses leaves the door open – whereas the first set of responses firmly closes the door. Some include positive speculation – if you are going to speculate, keep it positive, because this at least keeps the door open, whereas negative speculation does not.

Successful sales people:

- are curious about the behaviour patterns of their clients and prospects, rather than judgemental;
- hold back from placing meaning on their prospects' behaviour;
- flex their own behaviour patterns to match those of their clients and prospects, with a view to helping them make a decision;
- enjoy the journey of discovery;
- continue to learn more about the differences between people.

03

How your clients make decisions

You will now have a clear understanding of the importance of metaprogrammes in relationship building. Practise using this awareness to help your clients and prospects to make decisions. In this chapter we will explore the different ways in which your customers make decisions.

Gary's story

Gary sold top-of-the-range executive sports cars. His background was in engineering and he could not believe his luck when he landed a sales role that would mean he would be surrounded all day by such wonderful examples of fine engineering. He loved nothing more than to show his prospects under the bonnet of his cars and enthuse about horsepower, valves and cooling systems. He would start up the engine and rev happily, inviting his prospects to enjoy the throaty roar of his well-tuned vehicles. Gary found it easy to sell to fellow engine enthusiasts.

But, despite his natural enthusiasm, at the end of his probationary period Gary was invited into the manager's office and told he was not reaching his targets.

Gary's sales approach was only appealing to those people who processed information in an auditory/kinaesthetic way, similar to his own method of processing, i.e. the people who would be moved emotionally by the sound of the engine. Gary mistakenly believed that all his customers were going to be attracted to the sound and throb of a well-tuned engine. People whose first attraction was the look and/or feel of a car were being turned off, or perhaps I should say 'tuned out', by his approach. Such customers would hear him in the showroom and actively avoid him because they did not understand what he was talking about. Gary was unaware that a large percentage of the car-buying population make their decisions on the basis of what a car looks like and not what it sounds like. He was consequently placing severe restrictions on his potential market, selling only to those who shared his enthusiasm for the engine's characteristics.

How people make buying decisions through their senses

We all have different ways of filtering, processing and storing information through our five senses. Some people use their visual channel more readily, others their auditory channel and yet others their kinaesthetic channel (or feeling channel, as it is more commonly known). In the Western world these three channels are the most often used. In Eastern cultures the sense of smell and taste may come into play more, as they do in specific industries such as the food or perfume industry.

Understanding these channels and using them in the sales process can increase your success rate enormously. People use all their senses to process information and have what is known in NLP as a lead and/or preferred system. This means that when initially paying attention to something, a person may first visualise a picture (lead system) and then quickly access their feelings in relation to the picture (preferred system). In this example the lead system is the visual. Alternatively, like Gary in the story opposite, people may be drawn to the sound of an engine, in which case they are leading with their auditory channel. Let's explore these sensory systems and then look at utilising them to help more prospects become customers.

Visual processing

Visual processors are likely to be attracted by the look of a car – the shape, the colour, the style of the interior, the lights, the flashes on the side, the triangular exhaust pipes, the sleekness of the bonnet and so on. If the car does not look right they probably will not want to know anything else about it. If it does, then they may have a secondary processing preference, which could be, for example, auditory (sound of the engine),

kinaesthetic (feel of the bucket seats or soft leather upholstery) or even olfactory (smell of the leather upholstery). From
experience, people whose preference is for visual processing
represent approximately 35 per cent of the population. In
Gary's case, therefore, he was excluding 35 per cent of his
potential market by focusing his selling technique on the sound
of the engine.

How to recognise a visual processor

- Their eyes look upwards when thinking.

- They have fast, high-pitched speech. (Not always – this
  generally happens if people see moving pictures as opposed
  to still. The fast speech enables them to keep up with the
  movement of their pictures.)

- Their breathing is shallow.

- Their body posture when sitting and standing allows their eyes
  to look upwards – this can be disconcerting as it can appear
  relaxed and laid back and sometimes even far away.

- They use words and phrases such as: see, visualise, colour,
  shape, imagine, let me see, I can visualise, picture, diagram,
  flow chart, design, graph, flash, plainly see, get a perspective,
  sight for sore eyes, eye to eye, image, aspect, clear, horizon,
  focus, dim view, observe, tunnel vision, illustrate, hindsight,
  bright, perception, illusion, in view of, in light of, clear cut,
  vague, view, fuzzy edges, set the scene, cause a scene, look
  alike, foresee, stunning, gorgeous, fabulous, fantastic, see
  it happening, looking forward, take a view, sneak preview,
  bird's eye view, blue-sky thinking, watchful eye, see it through
  their eyes, take a long-term view, looks good, my view of this,
  take a different angle, see clearly, from all viewpoints, turn a
  blind eye, see the light, gives the appearance of, a colourful
  description, sees everything in black and white, the way I see
  it is.

- They will be drawn to the pictures and diagrams in a brochure or on a website.

- They will probably be dressed in carefully put together, colour co-ordinated clothes as their visual appearance is important to them. They may go so far as to dress in uncomfortable clothes and shoes as long as they look good.

- Their offices are often stylish and/or decorated with visual aids such as graphs, flow charts and pictures.

- They may spend what appears to be a long time staring out of the window while you are talking – possibly visualising how your products will work in their organisation.

- They may pick up a pencil or flip chart pen to 'draw out' what you are explaining.

- They may judge you on your appearance and/or the style of your car.

How to sell to a visual processor

- Match the pitch and pace of the voice as well as the visual language being used.

- Use diagrams, pictures and visual aids.

- Resist the temptation to talk when they are visualising – allow them time to complete the picture.

- Create pictures for them by using success stories involving your products and descriptive words that allow them to create pictures for themselves.

- Bear in mind that visual processors really need to 'see' in their mind's eye your products being used in their environment.

- Use hand gestures to draw the eyes upwards at appropriate times in the presentation to encourage visual processing.

Example

Jeff was a financial services sales executive. His client, Paul, was the CEO of a creative graphic design agency. Jeff knew that Paul would not be excited by the facts and figures of his services, even though he knew that he could save Paul thousands of pounds that were 'leaking' from his business. Jeff used water as a metaphor for the money that Paul was losing and 'painted' a picture of the water leaking from various points of the business – a picture that Paul was able to translate for himself using his visual processing. Jeff left the meeting with a signed contract.

Auditory processing

Auditory processors are sensitive to sound. They can make fine distinctions in sound – hence they are able to recognise a finely tuned engine or the different instrumental sounds in an orchestra. They are able to listen carefully to your solutions and process the information in an auditory way – often taking time to work things out mentally. You can make good progress on the telephone with these people. From experience, people with a preference for auditory processing make up approximately 20 per cent of the population.

How to recognise an auditory processor

- Their eye movements are likely to be sideways.
- Their eyes may appear narrow.
- Their voice tone is likely to be considered and melodic and their enunciation clear.
- They need to complete their sentences – they may become irritated if you don't allow this to happen.
- Their breathing comes from the mid abdomen.

- They may be sensitive to noises such as doors slamming, intrusive music, dripping taps, pen tapping and sniffing.

- They will use words and phrases such as: I hear what you are saying, I think we are singing from the same hymn sheet, music to my ears, give me a few sound bites, I'll have the one with all the bells and whistles, that sounds good, earful, earshot, pronounce, suggest, talk, speak, quiet, tone, tongue-tied, give an account of, lend an ear, idle talk, say, screams out for, pay attention to, describe in detail, communicate, tone, oral, noisy, can you comment on, grant an audience with, unheard of, word for word, mention, sound, shout, silence, lyrical, call, don't quote me, that rings a bell, bend his ear, hear me out, listen, let me tell you something, I don't like the sound of that, I like what I am hearing, am I hearing this correctly, up to my ears in, put in a word for, speaks for itself, turn up the volume.

- Their body posture is likely to be still and precise to allow sounds to penetrate.

- They will read out the descriptions of your products and services in a report or brochure and probably be happy to communicate by e-mail and telephone.

How to sell to an auditory processor

- Match the auditory words and phrases used, as well as the tone and pitch of the voice.

- Avoid distracting noises – for example, close doors carefully and keep still when presenting so as not to jangle keys or tap pens.

- Allow the auditory processor to complete sentences without interruption.

- Choose your words carefully and be precise.

- Remember that they will respond well to the written word as well as to the telephone – e-mail, reports, website information, schedules and specifications.

Kinaesthetic processing

Kinaesthetic processors use their feelings to make decisions. They can be either adversely sensitive to touch or like to be touched – for example, they may use an overly long handshake or put an arm round your shoulder. They are often referred to as intuitive as they 'feel' their way through the decision-making process. People with a preference for kinaesthetic processing make up approximately 45 per cent of the population.

How to recognise a kinaesthetic processor

- Their eyes look down, generally to the right when thinking (maybe to the left for a left-handed person).

- Their voice is likely to be deep.

- They use words and phrases such as: grasp, hard knocks, hard-headed, soft-headed, hold on, clutch, sharp, intuition, gut feeling, push, shove, smooth, hot-headed, solid, rock-hard, rock-solid, touch, warm, cold fish, tied up, pulling strings, bumpy ride, thumping headache, settled, bedding in, embedded, get a handle on, gripping story, jumping hurdles, getting round barriers, scraping by, sailing close to the wind, touch base, jumping through hoops, hard hitting, give it some welly, life of hard knocks, bounce ideas around, touch base, feel my way through, push his buttons, gut feeling, softly softly approach, suck it and see, grin and bear it, go the extra mile, put pressure on, push the boat out, take up the slack, things don't stack up, pull out all the stops, stressful, putty in his hands, keep cool, chill out, bend the rules, banging on about, hammer out a solution, sledge hammer to crack a nut, point the finger at, put through the mill, shudder to think, tug at the heart strings, not a shred of evidence, emotional response, carving a niche, removing the barriers, putting down roots, planting a seed.

- Their feelings are deep in the gut and it takes time to access them, therefore, they have plenty of time to breathe deeply.

- Their speech may be slower than the energetic speech of the visual processor. They may even drawl or be even in tone.

- They dress for comfort not style and may prefer an old sweater with a hole in the sleeve and comfy old corduroy trousers to anything else.

- They will sit in whatever way is most comfortable, even if this means lounging or turning the chair round to lean on the back.

- When buying, they will want to touch things and play with models and samples.

- They may fiddle with a pen or something similar, particularly if it has a nice feel to it.

- They may be attracted to your brochures because they have a nice feel to them rather than for the content or visual aspects.

How to sell to a kinaesthetic processor

- Reflect back the kinaesthetic words and phrases they use.

- Speak more slowly to enable the kinaesthetic processor to access their feelings – this is particularly important if you have a preference for visual processing with a tendency to speak quickly.

- Appeal to their feelings and emotion in relation to your products and services.

- Make sure the selling environment is a comfortable one.

- Don't assume they can visualise what you are talking about.

- If possible, take samples of your products to the sales presentation and let the kinaesthetic processor touch them or use them in some way.

- Be creative about the ways you can get these people doing, touching and experiencing things.

- Hold back from judging their appearance!

Example

Carol sells furniture to businesses in and around the north of England. She had been trying to get Ken, the buyer responsible for furnishing a small group of family hotels, to buy a lovely leather range of chairs and sofas for the reception halls. She showed him pictures from her catalogue and he was unmoved. When she asked him what he didn't like about the range, he said that in his experience leather was cold to sit on and he found it unfriendly. Realising Ken's kinaesthetic nature, Carol had a chair from the range sent to his office for a month. Ken loved the feel and warmth of it so much that he bought the range for the entire group.

Other senses

In industries and cultures where the sense of smell and taste are important, you may hear words and phrases such as 'I smell a rat', 'It leaves a bad taste in my mouth', 'This has the essence of something exciting', 'Can you give me a taste of what this might be like?'. Body gestures might include touching the nose or excessive swallowing. Smell and taste can play a large part in selling outside these industries as well.

Example

A friend of mine had the experience of a salesman from a well-established kitchen company calling at her house to design her new kitchen. He arrived smelling strongly of stale tobacco, a smell to which my friend has a particular aversion. She couldn't get him out of the house quick enough and needless to say he left without a sale. The sad thing is that she only has to hear the name of this company mentioned in an advertisement and the memory of this salesman and the smell comes back immediately.

Using all the senses

Of course, as I said at the beginning of this chapter, people use all their senses. For example, a person with a preference for visual processing may access their thoughts visually and then quickly move into kinaesthetic mode. We call this V-K processing. Similarly, a person with a preference for auditory processing may listen intently and then move into kinaesthetic mode and tell you how they feel about something. The purpose here is not to find a label for people but to learn to use what we call sensory acuity to monitor a person's processing from moment to moment. If we label a person as visual, the next time we meet them they may be having a kinaesthetic moment, having just heard a sad or touching story or having had a disagreement with a colleague or a loved one. The secret of success is to take what information is being offered in the moment (as shown in Figure 3.1) or, to use an NLP term, to calibrate the situation and respond to it accordingly.

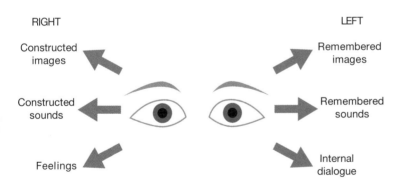

Figure 3.1 Eye accessing cues: note that this represents observing another person's accessing cues, i.e. remembered images are up to *their* left; it is also for a right-handed person – a left-hander may switch left with right

Developing sensory acuity

NLP practitioners practise their sensory acuity. This means they look for small signals that indicate a change of state in people. Whether or not your prospects are going to buy from you will depend upon the state – or in other words the state of mind the prospects are in. If what you have been saying has opened up their thinking in some way, this will show. They may take on a state of curiosity or reflection or they may gaze into the distance as they project an idea into the future based on what you have been saying. If you miss these signals, you may miss an opportunity to help them develop their ideas, or maybe you need to be still for a moment while they process their thinking.

Practise noticing small changes in your prospects as they go from one state to another. In Chapter 6 you will learn how to anchor positive states so that you can use them to bring your prospects back into a buying state.

Here are some things to look out for when someone is changing their state:

- change of posture;
- gazing into the distance;
- changes in the rate of breathing;
- voice tone;
- eye movements – up, down and sideways;
- pupil size;
- complexion changes – flushing, paling.

Learn to connect these state changes with what your prospect is saying so that when they are saying nothing you can accurately assess their state.

Focusing out

It is worth taking a moment here to emphasise the importance of focusing your attention outwards when dealing with clients. By this I mean paying full attention to what is being said, how the client is reacting and behaving, and noticing any body movements they make. All this gives an insight into how they are processing and will ultimately indicate when a prospect is ready to buy.

Your conscious attention is limited (see Figure 3.2), and in order to focus outwards it is important that you have prepared thoroughly so that you don't have to revert to internal dialogue, such as:

■ Did I bring the right brochures or order forms?

■ What am I going to say next?

■ Did I put any money in the parking meter?

■ Do I really know the key features of this particular product?

■ I left the samples in the car.

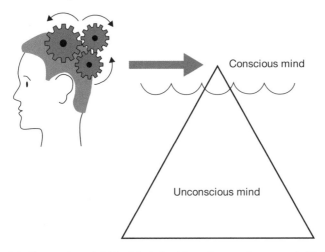

Figure 3.2 The conscious mind (tip of the iceberg) has a tiny capacity compared with that of the unconscious mind (the part of the iceberg underwater)

- What are they thinking?

- I hope they don't ask me any technical questions.

- What if I don't get this sale?

While your mind is occupied talking to yourself in this way, you will find yourself unable to use your sensory acuity to watch for key buying signals, or even hear what your prospect is saying.

Staying focused out

Try this exercise to help you stay focused outwards and to keep a mental note of what your client is saying so that you can refer back to it later.

1 Look up and create a strong colourful image in your mind of a notice board and of your hands placing sticky notes on the board.

2 As you concentrate on your prospect's conversation, pick out key words relating to something about which you would like more clarity, or would like to come back to later.

3 Mentally jot them down on separate sticky notes and place them on the board.

4 You will find yourself recalling these key words at an appropriate moment later in the conversation. Even if it turns out that you don't need them, the exercise will have kept you focused outwards.

Storing memories

Let's take a moment here to explore further how the mind stores information in the form of memories, because it is upon these memories that decisions are made. The mind is a bit like a filing cabinet – it has a location for certain types of memories.

Pleasant memories are stored in one location and unpleasant ones in another. To show you what I mean, try this.

1 Think of an unpleasant experience you have had in relation to your sales career – perhaps a presentation went wrong, or a client was particularly disparaging, or you said something you later regretted. Recall this specific incident and notice the qualities of the image:

- Is it in colour or black and white?
- If there is colour, are the colours muted, or is there one strong colour in particular?
- How far away is it – is it very close or some distance away?
- How defined is the picture – does it have fuzzy edges?
- Is it framed?
- Is there any movement?
- Can you hear anything?
- As you look at this image now, how does it make you feel? Do you sense a knot anywhere or a pain in a specific location – maybe a sense of sickness in the stomach or throat?

Change your position to discard the picture but keep in mind the qualities of the picture you have noticed.

2 Now think of a time when you were very successful – maybe you were signing a big contract or maybe you booked an appointment with someone you had been trying to engage with for some time. Again, be specific with the scenario you choose, and notice the qualities of the image by asking yourself the same questions as above.

Sometimes our images can become confused and we can store them in inappropriate places in the mind – this can lead to stress and maybe even depression – but on the whole the unconscious mind knows what to do and stores our images in places that work well for us. You probably noticed that your pleasant image was closer to you, you may even have been in the image, and the image was brighter in colour and more defined than the unpleasant image. Perhaps there were pleasant sounds and movement in the image. Your negative image, on the other hand, was probably further away, less colourful, maybe even a little blurred. The feelings associated with the pleasant image will no doubt be softer and warmer and have some good energy about them, whereas the very words we use to describe negative feelings, such as 'knot in the stomach' and 'lump in the throat', illustrate the negativity of such feelings. You could say that this ability to take the strength out of unpleasant images is the unconscious mind's way of looking after us – protecting us from unpleasant memories and keeping pleasant memories bright and colourful.

Try just one more thing to really prove the point:

■ Recall your negative image – bring it close, put some colour into it, turn up the sounds and make it really clear. Notice how the negative feelings get stronger as you do so. Return the image to where it was.

■ Recall your pleasant image – turn down the colour, push it away and turn the volume down on the sound. Notice how your unconscious mind does not want this to happen and the image wants to spring back to its rightful place, making you feel good.

Later on in the book we shall use this ability to play with our images to create new ways of thinking, new behaviour patterns and new success strategies. For now, practise becoming aware of how and where you store your negative and positive images and how moving them about can significantly change the way you feel.

Successful sales people:

■ know that people process information differently inside their heads;

■ know that people will warm to them unconsciously if they learn to match their processing system;

■ know that they can widen their potential market by learning to match different processing methods;

■ know that heightened sensory acuity will help them recognise changes in state;

■ know that it is important to prepare well so that they can stay focused outwards;

■ know that whether or not their prospect buys from them will depend on the prospect's physiological state – it is up to the sales person to help create a state for buying.

04

Aligning with your role, your clients and your organisation

If you are to lead a successful sales career, it is important for you to make sure that you can align yourself with the values and practices of your organisation, as well as with the requirements of your role and your potential clients. Such alignment will enable you to carry out your role with integrity and commitment.

Carl's story

Carl had been selling high-quality printing for many years. He was good at his job and often won industry awards for his achievements. As digital printing became popular and the industry became more computerised, Carl was convinced that the conventional print industry was dying. The impact of this one belief was devastating. He stopped trying. His focus completely changed. He began noticing all the prospects who did not buy from him and the long-term customers who were cancelling. When he visited the customers he retained, his attitude had changed – he was morose and complained about the state of the industry. He slowly lost more and more clients.

Fortunately, Carl was able to turn his fortunes around. When it was pointed out to him just what a powerful effect this one belief was having on his performance, he reversed the belief to: 'The industry is changing, our company can change with it and I can change the way I sell.' Carl went back to prospects and clients that he had virtually written off and within just a few weeks he was back on track with his sales targets and his career.

The ancient Hawaiians had a saying that 'Energy flows where attention goes'. By focusing on the negative side of his role, his potential business and his activities, Carl had been wasting a great deal of energy that he could have been putting into developing new, more positive and productive relationships.

Are you fully aligned with what you are doing?

Often sales people are unsuccessful in their role because they are not fully aligned with it. Take a look at Figure 4.1.

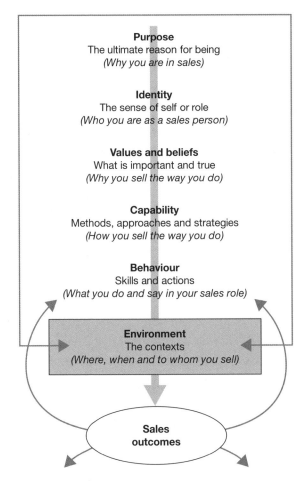

Figure 4.1 The alignment model

This model is known as the alignment model, or neurological levels of learning, communication and change. It helps us to understand the human processes of learning, communication and change and is generally accredited to Robert Dilts (although the original research was conducted by an English anthropologist called Gregory Bateson). It suggests that we perform these three functions on different levels, with each level affecting the level(s) below. If we want to create change at the level of capability, for example, then we may need to do some work at one or more of the levels above, i.e. values and beliefs, identity or purpose. Ultimately, changes at any level will impact the environment in which we function.

Let's take a look at each level and its implications for you as a sales person.

Purpose

What is the purpose of you selling this product? Take your time to really think about it. Is it:

- To earn as much commission as you can?
- To keep your directors/colleagues/family happy?
- To improve the profitability of your customer?
- To prove something to yourself?
- To beat your own sales record?
- To beat your fellow sales executives?
- To improve the environment?
- To help other people to achieve?
- To keep the wolf away from the door?
- Something else?

Whatever you perceive your purpose to be will impact how you see your role as a sales person. For example, if you see your purpose as to earn as much commission as you possibly can so that you can buy the luxuries in life, then you may see your role as a money accumulator and develop a set of values and beliefs to support this role. On the other hand, you may see your purpose as being to improve the profitability of your customer, in which case you may see your role more as a facilitator designing solutions to fulfil this purpose. Here, too, you will develop a set of values and beliefs to support this role.

Identity (or role)

How do you see yourself as a sales person? It could be as:

- a facilitator
- a conqueror
- a supporter
- an informer
- a competitor in a race
- a provider
- a front-line person
- an expert.

How does this compare with other roles in your organisation? Are they more important, less important or of equal importance? Are you a team player recognising that you need the support of your organisation, or do you think the organisation should keep up with you?

Being able to describe your role will help you to identify what is really important to you. For example, as a facilitator you are more likely to value the input from your prospects and work with them to find solutions to their buying issues. As a conqueror, on the other hand, you are more likely to see your prospect as someone who needs to be won over – someone who possibly does not know what they need. As a challenger in a race, you may value the competition with your colleagues more than the input from your prospects.

Values and beliefs

If you can answer the question, 'What is important to you about sales?' then this is a value you hold. See if you can answer this question now.

Here are some suggestions of things that may be important to you:

- Your client receives a fair deal.

- Your products are top class.

- Other people value your products.

- Your clients receive quality after-sales service.

- You drive a top-of-the-range motor and use the latest mobile phone.

- You can work autonomously.

- You get to travel.

- You can arrange your hours around your social life.

- You receive recognition from your company.

- Something else.

Knowing what is important to you will determine whether or not you seek out the means to fulfil these values. For example, if your client receiving a fair deal is important to you, then you will probably research the possibilities within your own company and compare them with the competition. If selling top-class products is important to you, then you will make sure that you work with an organisation that produces these and be very uncomfortable anywhere else.

In Chapter 2 we looked at the impact that some meta-programmes have on your behaviour, as well as that of your prospects and clients, and how these can affect your results. Metaprogrammes can be considered as values. Here are some examples of values generated by metaprogrammes:

- Giving the prospect all the information available (detail).

- Completing the process from beginning to end (procedures).

- Making sure that the prospect is aware of all the options (options).

- Keeping meetings on schedule (through time).

- Pointing out all the 'security'-based features (away from).

- Needing recognition by your company or client (external reference).

Knowing that you have a strong metaprogramme in place is important for when you meet someone with the opposite meta-programme. For example, if your preference is for detail and you meet someone with the opposite pattern who tries to get you to hurry along a bit, it is important that you do not misinterpret this as disinterest. This person may be telling you that they like the idea of your product but do not really need all the detail at this stage. Similarly, if you have a tendency towards security and you are selling to someone with a towards pattern, they may appear to disregard your implied warnings. Again, this is not that they do not value your approach, it's just that their approach is different.

Example

Bob had a high value around material things. He took a job as a luxury goods sales person because it included a top-of-the range BMW, the latest mobile phone and a super-duper laptop. He did not bother to check out the quality of the organisation's product range before taking the job, although he also had a high value around customer satisfaction. During his first week in the role Bob quickly became aware of the poor quality of his product range. At first he was prepared to disregard this, such was the pull of his car, phone and laptop. It was not long, however, before Bob felt a real emotional tug because his values were being compromised. He could not continue selling such a poor-quality product and he left the company very soon after joining.

Closely aligned with your values will be a set of beliefs. For example, if it is important to you that your client receives a fair deal, then you will have strong beliefs around the quality of your product, its competitiveness and its appropriateness for this particular client. If that is not important then you may not hold these beliefs. If it is important but you do not hold these beliefs, then you are going to feel that tug again, and your discomfort will show to your prospect. You are unlikely to succeed in a role where misalignments such as these exist.

Ask yourself what you believe about your role in sales. Is it one of the following?

- My products/services are paramount.
- My products are competitively priced.
- Our company offers excellent after-sales service.
- Our company can deliver on time.
- The customer needs time to consider.
- The customer must be closed down as quickly as possible.
- Customers won't sign until they have all the facts.
- Some prospects procrastinate forever and will never sign.
- Customers are difficult.
- Customers are great – they just need careful handling.
- Selling is hard work.
- Selling is fun.
- I can't sell that range of products – it is too expensive.
- Customers never answer the phone.
- The economic climate is making people hold back on buying.
- There is a market out there, despite the economic climate.
- Something else.

Check out your beliefs about individual customers. For example:

- Gary Black cancelled the meeting last week: he's not interested.

- Paul will cancel the order when I tell him it's going to be three weeks late.

- If we put the price up we will lose the Nifty Engineering Company as a client.

- Sally won't buy this in a million years; she's too set in her ways.

Beliefs have a habit of creeping up on us. They come from a childhood desire to find a reason or meaning for things that happen to us. In your early years you will have most likely adopted some of the beliefs that your parents and siblings held. Later on you will have gathered some of those offered by school friends, teachers and icons. In your working life someone may have disregarded something you said on one occasion and this has transformed into the belief that 'She never listens to anything I say'. This is, of course, ridiculous but it may take only one incident for a belief to take shape and become embedded. Imagine how you would behave if you held the belief that 'She never listens' about a prospect. Perhaps you would:

- put her to the bottom of your contact list;

- fail to prepare thoroughly for your meeting with her;

- get the meeting over as quickly as possible;

- not bother contacting her at all.

In fact, unconsciously, you will probably do everything you need to do to prove you are right. This is how beliefs work – you form a core belief, and then look for and focus on evidence to prove it, thus attracting similar beliefs to your core belief and ignoring evidence to the contrary.

Think of the link between your beliefs and values as a tree (see Figure 4.2 overleaf). The roots of the tree represent your core beliefs, and the trunk represents your values, holding your core beliefs in place and feeding the fruit of the tree, i.e. the other beliefs attracted to your core beliefs.

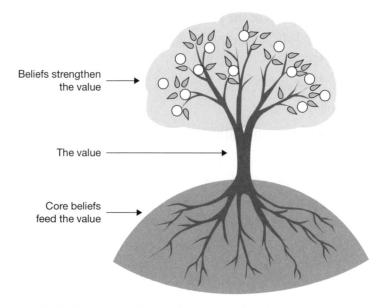

Beliefs strengthen
the value →

The value →

Core beliefs
feed the value →

Figure 4.2 The link between beliefs and values

Some beliefs are empowering while others are limiting, as shown in the example above. Whatever you believe about your role, your products, your customers and your company will have a direct impact on your capability as a sales person. It would be a shame to think that much higher earnings potential was being stifled by a limiting core belief, wouldn't it?

Take some time to reflect on your own beliefs about:

- your company;
- your product/service range;
- your ability to sell;
- your customers/prospects;
- your industry;
- the impact your beliefs about the above has on your family and friends.

In the next chapter we shall take a closer look at the language patterns that indicate the presence of beliefs. Knowing how to recognise and challenge your own limiting beliefs and those of your prospects and clients will help to improve your success rate in sales.

Capability (or potential)

Some people are naturally talented sales people. They appear to have the gift of the gab and make themselves appealing to everyone they meet. Others need to spend time developing their skills, turning their potential into real ability. Whether or not you do this will depend on what is important to you and whether or not you believe it is possible.

If something is important to you and you believe it can happen, then you will focus on ways to make it happen. If it is not important or you do not believe it, then you will not look and things will remain the same. So, based on what you have decided is important to you and having checked out your beliefs around these values, what skills do you need to fulfil them? How much untapped potential do you have? Here are some suggestions for what you might need:

- rapport-building skills
- organisational skills
- communication skills
- influencing skills
- persistence
- creativity
- listening skills
- open-mindedness
- empathy
- courage

- telephone skills
- patience
- determination
- flexibility
- analytical skills
- industry knowledge
- product knowledge
- people knowledge.

Score yourself out of 10 on each of the above areas and decide how you are going to bring yourself closer to 10 in those areas where you know you fall short. Review your last five prospect meetings and ask yourself if a shortfall in any of these areas was the reason why you did not agree a deal.

Behaviour

Often behaviour becomes habitual, based upon what is important to us and what we believe. Without a challenge, such habitual behaviour will continue to be enacted, so it makes sense to ensure that our values are strong and our beliefs are empowering.

When you have addressed the shortfalls at the capability level, your behaviour will change. For example, if you decide you could increase your capacity to listen more carefully then you will find yourself doing more listening and less speaking. You may find your creativity increases as a result of formulating ideas from what you hear, and that more and varied solutions are brought to the table.

If you develop your ability to empathise, for example, you may start to see things more clearly from your prospect's point of view and modify your behaviour accordingly.

Whatever it is you lack, remember that you are in control and it is up to you to make the necessary changes that will impact your results. The minute you begin to blame other factors, such as the market, the economic climate or changes in the industry, then you have handed control over to something or someone other than yourself and you will develop the same feeling of helplessness that Carl did in the story earlier.

Example

Greg inherited his father's jewellery business. Both Greg and his father continued to work in the business. Greg wanted to specialise in high-priced items such as diamond engagement rings. However, when he was not in the shop his father continued to accept low-value alterations, promising the delivery and service his clientele had come to expect. Greg did not value these customers and would put his high-value customers first, regardless of what his father had promised. Delivery dates slipped and with them went Greg's reputation as a businessman. His misalignment between what he believed the company should be doing and what was actually happening impaired the performance of the business. Fortunately, Greg sought help from a business coach and was able to get the company's performance back on track using a new business model that both he and his father were able to buy into.

It is not uncommon to hear people say of their behaviour, 'I can't help it – it just comes out that way' or 'I always do that', even though they know it is not getting the results they require. Habitual behaviour is more likely to show itself in times of stress; so, for example, if you are normally a fast speaker you will be able to consciously slow down for a while, but as soon as the going gets tough then your speech will tend to return to its normal fast pace. This is because you have not embedded your new behaviour successfully from the start. To develop a new behaviour you need to see what it looks like if you were to do it, and then you need to rehearse it regularly.

Generating a new behaviour

Here is a technique for generating a new behaviour:

1 Identify the new behaviour you would like to have – for example, you may want to:

   - flex your procedural approach;

   - offer only one or two solutions instead of the many you have been used to;

   - offer a bigger-picture approach;

   - spend longer building rapport;

   - become more organised;

   - be more confident using the telephone;

   - develop the skill of listening with positive intent;

   - improve your timekeeping/record keeping/report writing;

   - improve something else.

2 Sit quietly somewhere and, with your eyes down, ask yourself what it would be like if you were to indulge in this new behaviour.

3 Now look up and create a picture of yourself actually doing this new thing. Create the picture at a short distance from yourself and put a frame around it. Make it clear and bright, adding in any sounds and movements that may be appropriate.

4 When the picture is clear, bring it forward so that you can mentally step into it and feel what it is like to be successful at this new behaviour.

5 If this is a feeling of success that you recognise from other successful areas of your life, then repeat the exercise several times to really burn in the new behaviour.

6 If you don't recognise the feelings as those of success, go back to step 3 and repeat the exercise, adding in anything that might be missing – this may be some internal resources such as

patience, confidence, awareness or it may be that you need to develop a new skill. Whatever it is, see yourself including this in your picture before going on to the next step.

Once you have designed your new behaviour in this way, you need to practise it at every opportunity until it becomes a new habit – so you can draw on it unconsciously without having to think about it.

Environment

The new behaviours you develop will have an impact on those around you. If you become a good listener, your prospects will begin to think that you really understand them and want to help them. If you show more empathy, the same will happen and you will begin to complete more deals. As you complete more deals, more people will want to emulate your success and you will attract more attention from colleagues and clients and more referrals. Your self-esteem will increase and as this happens so your success rate will multiply.

The importance of being aligned

Here is another presupposition of NLP:

You cannot not *communicate.*

Misalignments in sales people are easy to spot – they come across as insincerity, stubbornness, a lack of caring or maybe disinterest. Body language, tone of voice and facial expressions are all key indicators. Try it for yourself: try to be enthusiastic about something that you really believe is rubbish – a TV programme, for example, or a film you did not enjoy, a book you have just read or maybe someone at work you really do not get on well with. Listen to your voice tone as you describe this person or thing. How does the way you are speaking differ from when you are naturally enthusiastic about things? Ask your friends and colleagues if they can tell the difference.

Equally, if you do not begin the sales process by believing from every angle that you are going to make a sale and maintain this belief throughout, you will communicate this to your prospect – and lo and behold you will lose the sale. Take some time to check how aligned you are in all areas of your role as a sales executive. What is your purpose? How do you see your role? What is important to you and what do you believe about all aspects of your role? What skills are you lacking? How does this affect what you do and finally what impact are you having on those around you?

Once you have done this, consider whether you are aligned with the company you represent. If you are misaligned in some way, decide whether or not you can live with it or whether the misalignment is so strong that you would be better looking elsewhere for a place to utilise your skills. If you are aligned then congratulate yourself and continue doing a great job.

Pacing and leading

NLP teaches us to build rapport with a client and then to elegantly pace and lead them towards a well-formed outcome that is mutually beneficial to both parties. Pacing is the process of using what you know about your prospect, what they tell you and how they tell you to gain their confidence. This can include their values, beliefs, past experience, metaprogrammes, processing channels, body language and product and personal information. In general, twice as much pacing as leading is recommended in a new relationship. As the relationship gets stronger, you will find you will not need quite so much pacing.

An example of inelegant pacing may go something like this:

Prospect: We have had a terrible month.

Sales person: Yes, so have we.

In this example the sales person is using their own perspective – or, as it is called in NLP, their own map of the world – in order to communicate. In fact the reality is that the prospect is unlikely to be interested in the sales person's perspective, and the sales person's response does nothing to take the conversation forward.

An example of elegant pacing may go like this:

Prospect: We have had a terrible month.

Sales person: Oh really – what do you think has caused it to be terrible?

Here the sales person is exploring the prospect's map and is in a position to gain more useful information, which may help with the sale.

Throughout this book you will be encouraged to use various techniques to pace your prospects and clients. You can begin to lead your client towards a mutually beneficial outcome once you are sure you have gained their confidence, using an appropriate amount of pacing.

Pacing and leading with the alignment model

You can use the alignment model to pace and lead your prospects and clients. Learn to ask questions at every level of the model to establish where your prospect is coming from. For example:

■ What is the purpose behind you exploring these new products [purpose]?

■ What are you aiming to achieve here [purpose]?

■ Are you the decision maker or is there someone else involved [identity]?

- How will these products affect you personally [identity]?
- What is important to you about these products [values]?
- What criteria do they have to fulfil [values]?
- What do you believe will happen if you try these products [beliefs]?
- What do you believe will happen if you don't try these products [beliefs]?
- Are there any other areas in the business that would benefit from these products [capability]?
- Who will be using these products [behaviour]?
- How do you see people using them [behaviour]?
- How will these products impact your business [environment]?

The following chapters will take a closer look at the aspects of alignment mentioned above and offer some further tools and techniques for making changes.

Successful sales people:

- align themselves with the neurological levels of learning, communication and change, resulting in increased confidence, self-esteem and success;
- know that misalignments cause a feeling of discomfort, can impair performance and have an adverse effect on customer relationships;
- know that you cannot *not* communicate;
- identify areas for improvement and change at the capability level and create new behaviours accordingly;
- develop strong values and empowering beliefs;
- make sure they are aligned with the company they represent;
- pace and lead their clients using the alignment model.

05

Believing your way to success

In the previous chapter you learnt how important it is to believe in what you are doing and your ability to succeed. What you believe about yourself, your company and your prospects and clients will play a major part in determining your levels of success. In this chapter we will explore patterns of language that indicate underlying beliefs and look at ways to gain clarity around such beliefs.

Anne's story

Anne's company was experiencing a great deal of change. Tensions were high and people were feeling the strain of new systems, new roles and new management styles. When questioned about her environment, Anne described it as hostile and unfriendly. She had developed defensive coping strategies in her sales role – making sure she did not get 'caught out' by her managers, struggling to get her reports and sales records in on time and focusing on achieving sales come what may. In fact, so strong was her belief in the hostile environment that her defensive activities took precedence over her sales activities. She began to miss her targets as slowly her customers lost faith in her, perceiving her as unprepared, anxious and pushy.

Be careful what you believe

Anne's story demonstrates just how powerful negative or limiting beliefs can be. Had she believed her organisation to be supportive and encouraging rather than hostile, then her approach could have been very different. If you are going to continue to be successful in sales then it is important that you develop and maintain empowering not limiting beliefs. As we saw in the previous chapter, limiting beliefs have a direct impact on your capability, which in turn impacts your behaviour and therefore your results. So irrespective of whether Anne's organisation was supportive or not, Anne's choice to believe that it was not sent her down a negative route of behaviour that led to poor results.

Filtering information

From a very early age we have a desire to put meanings to the things that happen to us or the things that people say. 'Why?' is one of the first questions that we learn to ask: 'Why can't I play with my friends?', 'Why is he allowed to go and I can't?', 'Why does he get more pocket money than me?', 'Why do people die?', 'Why do my friends have two parents and I only have one?', 'Why is grass green and the sky blue?' – the list is endless as we develop an insatiable desire to fulfil our inquisitiveness. Sometimes we receive useful or practical answers and sometimes not; sometimes we don't receive answers at all and have to provide them for ourselves.

The human mind becomes adept at putting meanings on to the things that happen to us – often meanings that have no foundation in reality. Depending on whether these meanings are positively or negatively charged, they will have either a positive or a negative effect on our habitual thinking and behaviour.

Let's take a look at some examples:

- She said she didn't like the colour pink, so she will never buy our products.

- They have been buying from the Two Big Chaps Company for years, so I don't suppose they will ever change.

- Nobody will ever be able to understand the utility of this new product [unspoken meaning – they won't buy it].

- Our sales figures are down on last year [unspoken meaning – we are not doing very well].

- If I don't meet my targets, I will be out of a job.

- I must be careful what I say: he has a PhD and is much cleverer than me.

Of course these statements are only a manifestation of someone's take on a particular set of circumstances. As thoughts, they have no form or reality other than inside the person's head, but it is the meaning that you put on the things that happen to you that will determine any action you take, which of course will impact your results. It makes sense, therefore, to refrain from placing negative meanings in this way and to develop instead the habit of remaining open to other possibilities. For example:

- She said she didn't like the colour pink, but the benefits of this product may outweigh her dislike for the colour. Maybe we could even consider producing it in blue.

- They have been buying from the Two Big Chaps Company for years – I wonder what it is that the Two Big Chaps Company does so well? Perhaps we can improve on this.

- How can I make this simple for people to understand?

- Our sales figures are down on last year – but we are still here with much improved efficiencies. Next year we will focus on building our sales back up.

- What can I do to generate sales outside my normal channels?

- He is academically very clever but needs my practical approach in order to be able to really benefit from this product.

It is useful at this stage to take a look at the process of communication that we have been discussing so far – as shown in Figure 5.1.

The model tells us that, of the masses of information being received into the human mind at any one time, we can only process approximately five to nine pieces at once. Think of the mind as being in two parts – a very small part that handles

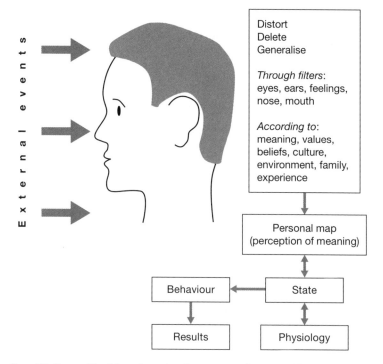

Distort
Delete
Generalise

Through filters:
eyes, ears, feelings,
nose, mouth

According to:
meaning, values,
beliefs, culture,
environment, family,
experience

Personal map
(perception of meaning)

Behaviour ← State

Results   Physiology

External events

Figure 5.1 How we filter information and produce our own unique map of the world

conscious activity and a considerably bigger part that handles unconscious activity or what we call habits. We will refer to these as the conscious mind and the unconscious mind. One of the functions of the conscious mind is to decide what to select to put into the unconscious mind to become a habit.

At this stage, the mind can choose either an empowering way of thinking or a limiting one. It does this very quickly through the sensory filters, taking account of such things as the metaprogramme profile, personal values and beliefs, personal experience and geographical and cultural influences. This whole process causes the conscious mind to delete, distort and generalise the messages being received at any one moment and the filtered thought sequence is the one that gets stored in the unconscious mind.

What people say and do is the last stage of the process and an excellent indicator of the thinking that has taken place in order to arrive at such behaviour. Habitual negative thinking will create habitual negative behaviour. Similarly, habitual positive thinking is more likely to result in habitual positive behaviour. This is a very simplistic description and if it was as simple as recognising positive and negative then everyone would be able to switch from one to the other without too much effort. Unfortunately, the process is largely unconscious and often people do not recognise their own limitations. Sometimes, even if they do, they believe their way of thinking is the right way and will go a long way to defend it, thus protecting their own limitations.

Example

Richard sells hair treatment products into hairdressing salons. The products were developed initially for women and Richard built his success around selling into upmarket ladies' salons. His area was a wide one and he travelled many miles in his work. Richard earned a good living, he had some nice customers with whom he had built strong business relationships and he settled into a very acceptable routine.

In the meantime, the market for male hairdressing products had taken off. Men's salons everywhere were buying hairdressing products, which Richard's company began to supply. Richard, however, treated the new products as faddish and outside his needs in relation to his current client base. Had he not been so engrained in his habitual behaviour, Richard would have realised that many of the men's salons, his prospective clients, were right next door to his current clients. He could have doubled the number of clients and therefore his sales, while halving his travelling.

Questioning limiting beliefs

The language structures people use are the same, whether they are used positively or negatively. For example, the following two statements follow the same structure:

■ Everyone is really happy with the new structure in the organisation.

■ Everyone is really disgruntled with the new structure in the organisation.

The statements may be describing the same organisational restructure, but they are from the perspectives of two different people and so are likely to elicit significantly different responses from the listener. The first response may cause the listener to believe that no action is necessary. The second may cause the listener to do some investigative work to find out what is wrong.

Milton Erickson was a therapist who used positive forms of the structures to pace and lead people from a negative frame of mind to a more productive one. These patterns became known as Miltonian patterns.

Learning to recognise and use these patterns in sales can serve two very powerful purposes:

■ To enable you to gain clarity around your own and your client's/prospect's thinking.

■ To pace and lead your prospect/client and win their commitment to buying your products and services. (This will be discussed further in Chapter 8.)

Other business contexts in which this technique can be used include coaching and motivating your team, writing great marketing and advertising material, communicating new ideas and concepts, and gaining clarity around complex situations.

In the following examples I will contextualise the patterns used negatively, thus suggesting a limitation in the sales environment, and offer a selection of questions you may wish to ask yourself or your client in order to shake the limitation. You can of course transfer the learning here to just about any other context.

In its haste to make sense of the world, your mind will choose to delete, distort or generalise the information it receives. Take a look at the statements that follow and see how questioning can change thinking.

People won't buy at this high price [deletion].

The speaker has omitted to tell us which people, what it is they are talking about and what they are comparing the 'high' price to. Unfortunately, the natural response to this can often be a defensive one – 'It's not high' or 'Yes, they will!'

A more productive approach would be to ask questions in order to gain some clarity around the speaker's thinking and help them find a solution. Here are some examples:

- By 'people', I take it you mean your current market – can you describe your client profile for me?
- When you say 'high', can you give me an idea of what you are measuring it against?
- How do you see this product? [May get the speaker to realise the value.]
- Can you give me an idea of what price you think your customers would pay for it?
- If your customers don't buy this product, what do you think they might buy instead?
- Can you think of examples where similar clients are paying a similar price for a comparable product? [Encourages a search for counter-evidence.]

Such questions will lead the speaker to review their thinking and entertain the idea that there are other ways of thinking about the product. The questions will also give you an opportunity to change your approach as a sales person, depending on the answers you receive.

Of course, as a sales person, you may have found yourself thinking something similar about products in your own range. If you have, take yourself back to that time and recall what you did. Maybe you put the product to the bottom of your priority list, or only introduced it to certain customers where you felt on safe ground. Looking back, how did this impact your results? Did others succeed with the product where you did not? Could you have done something different in order to generate more sales with this product? What made you think this way in the first place? Is the source of this thinking still valid? If faced with something like this again, what could you do differently?

We can't be a valued customer if you can't get the product to us in time for the exhibition [distortion].

In this case the speaker has placed a meaning on the timing of the delivery, which may or may not be correct. If they continue to believe that 'We can't be a valued customer', this is going to have a negative effect on any future relationship you may have. Some questions to ask are:

■ Let me see, the exhibition is in three weeks' time [highlighting the short timescale]. What if we can stagger the delivery so that you receive 50 per cent in time for the exhibition and the remainder a week later?

■ How does this compare with other deliveries we have made to you?

■ How does this compare with the delivery times of our competitors?

▪ What would you like us to do to show you that we value your custom?

We really must have the brochures by 16 December [deletion].

Whenever you hear the words must, have to or need, this is an indication that the speaker may have a procedural pattern and is restricting their thinking within the confines of the process. Your role here is to help the speaker to think more widely:

▪ What else will the visitors to your stand need?

▪ Is there anything else we can do to promote the products besides the brochures?

▪ If we didn't have them in time, what else can we do to make sure the exhibition is a success?

Every time we do an exhibition, it's a lot of work with absolutely no return [generalisation].

Here the speaker is being emphatic about the success of exhibitions by using what we call 'universal quantifiers' such as every and absolutely. Approaching an event in this frame of mind is not going to be productive and as a sales person you may wish to ask yourself the following questions:

▪ Do I really mean every time?

▪ Can I think of an occasion when we did benefit? [This may not have been immediately – it could have been several months later.]

▪ Is the exhibition useful for raising brand awareness?

▪ Is it an opportunity to learn what is going on in the industry?

▪ How am I defining a return?

▪ Have I set any personal outcomes for the exhibition?

▪ Are there any other outcomes I could take into account?

▪ How will I know when I have achieved them?

▪ How can I ensure that I absolutely do achieve them?

Selling is a numbers game (deletion).

Here the speaker has omitted to state the source of their statement – in other words, 'Who says so?' Believing this may restrict your success rate, so here are some questions to ask yourself:

- Where did I get this belief from?
- What kind of a numbers game?
- Does the industry I am in justify this type of thinking?
- Are the numbers still the same as they were when I first took on this belief?
- What other type of game could it be?
- Is it a game at all?
- How else could I think about selling, other than it being a game?
- If I reduced the numbers and focused on long-term relationships, how would this affect my results?

I know you won't like this product – it doesn't fit with the range [distortion].

In this example the speaker is attempting to read someone's mind. It usually occurs as a result of assumptions made from previous experience. It could be, and very often is, wrong. Some key questions could explore other possible ways of thinking:

- We have something a little different for you – I'd be interested to hear your opinion on this product?
- Your opinion of our products is valuable to us – can I ask you what you think of this? Can you see a market for it? [This question allows the client to voice an opinion without the need to fit the product into their own range.]

I'm fed up with sales people [generalisation].

A statement like this is usually based on a recent unpleasant experience. The speaker has generalised this experience across all sales people. Your role is to distance yourself from what has caused the comment, and your ability to do this is key to your success here:

- I'm sorry to hear that. What has happened to cause you to feel like this? [Depending on the response, reassure the speaker that you are different.]
- That's certainly not how a professional should behave – let me reassure you that we are very different from that. [You are isolating the experience and using the word 'that' to put distance between you and the offending sales person.] In fact, when you do business with us, x, y and z will happen [the opposite].

I've been using this product for a week and it doesn't work properly [deletion].

Here the speaker has omitted to define how exactly the product doesn't work. One of the worst things you can do as a sales person is to tell them that all your other customers are happy with it. This will simply serve to isolate your customer in a negative frame.

Some things you can ask to gain clarity around the problem include:

- I'm sorry to hear that – can you tell me what happens when you try to use it?
- Can you take me through the process you are applying?
- What would it look like if the product was working well for you?

All these questions focus on a solution to the problem, rather than a justification for it, and are more likely to result in a satisfied customer.

We are performing so badly this year [deletion].

This statement fails to tell us exactly *how* we (the speaker) are performing badly and could be wrongly taken to mean that the speaker is not in a position to buy right now. With some precision questioning around what exactly the speaker means, a way forward can be found. Some useful questions would be:

- Which aspects of performance do you mean?
- Is it all areas of performance or some isolated ones – sales, productivity, research, profitability, recruitment, training, learning and development, investment?
- If you were performing well, what exactly would that look like?
- All year? Was performance any better in some months?

Such questions will give you an opportunity to focus your pitch on areas where your products can enhance performance. Learning to use questions in this way to determine the underlying thinking of the speaker will greatly enhance your ability to pace and lead your prospective client or customer to a mutually beneficial sale.

Challenging limiting beliefs

So far, we have looked at questions you can ask when you come across limiting beliefs in your sales environment to help move you and other people forward. But how often do you challenge your own limiting beliefs? Beliefs about your clients, your capabilities, your products, the market you are in, the company you work for? We have already seen how negative beliefs result in negative behaviour, which will more often than not create negative results. However firmly you believe something to be negative, it is often a good idea to test out alternative beliefs for a while, just to see if you get a different result.

Try shaking your belief first by using the following series of questions:

1 When did I first develop this belief?

2 Where did it come from?

3 Do I know other people who share this belief?

4 Do I know other people who do not share this belief?

5 In what way is it limiting my progress?

6 In what way is the belief ridiculous or absurd?

7 What evidence do I have to support this belief?

8 What evidence is there to the contrary?

9 What will happen if I continue with this belief?

10 What might happen if I change it?

By now there should be some doubt around what you used to believe, and so you can design a better, more empowering belief. Here is an example of a limiting belief, followed by answers to the above questions, which allow you to move on to a more empowering belief.

- **Limiting belief**: This customer is never going to buy our products.

    1 I have visited this person four times and they have never bought anything from me.

    2 My own experience of this prospect.

    3 Yes, Bill in the Outerwear department believes this too.

    4 Yes, Sally in Separates and Rowena in Accessories both sell regularly to this client.

    5 I keep postponing appointments and my approach is quite negative.

    6 Other people are selling to this client – there is absolutely no reason why they should not buy my products.

    7 Only hearsay from Bill, who does not have a particularly good sales record.

8 Sally and Rowena are successful and I know that the client buys similar products to mine from another company.

9 I will continue to approach this customer in a negative frame of mind, which will be transparent to them and I will not gain the sales I am looking for.

10 I could build a positive business relationship with this person and increase my sales significantly.

▪ **More empowering belief**: This is a very discerning customer and I need to find a way to show them the benefits of our products. Perhaps if I have a word with Sally and Rowena: they may have some advice for me.

Ridding yourself of negative thinking

Sometimes your beliefs can be so engrained that raising awareness of their limiting nature and telling yourself that you are going to think differently in future is not enough. You start out with good intentions, find yourself in a similar situation again and the old behaviour returns. A technique you may find useful for changing your behaviour for ever is the swish technique.

Negative images can appear very fast and the feelings related to them can be extremely profound, even though the event has occurred some time ago. The swish technique can be used to change the way you think about things when you have had a negative experience. For example, in the sales context these may include picking up the telephone (particularly if your role involves some cold calling), speaking to a particularly difficult customer, making presentations or maybe delivering bad news.

Example

Jenny was a co-presenter with Bob working for a large IT company. They developed a successful formula for presenting different parts of the sales presentation. One day they were invited to give a presentation at an industrial conference and were allocated time slots of 15 minutes each to do so. Bob arrived agitated and unprepared – he asked if he could go first, stepped on to the stage to the PowerPoint presentation and proceeded to give Jenny's well-prepared presentation. When it came to Jenny's turn to present, she had nothing to say and floundered her way through the presentation. This experience stayed with Jenny, affecting her performance every time she was asked to present to large groups – until she learnt the swish technique.

Using the swish technique

1 Sit somewhere quietly where you can relax on your own for a short time.

2 Bring to mind the negative experience – this will bring up the negative feelings as well, but go along with the exercise knowing that it will have an excellent outcome for you.

3 Bring the picture right in front of you and put a mental frame around it.

4 Make it big and make it bright, turning up any sounds you can hear and being aware of the negative sensations you are experiencing.

5 Now put this image to one side for a moment – you will need it again soon.

6 Now think of something you would like to replace this image with. It can either be related directly to the negative one or be something completely different. The important thing here is that it is stronger in its positive nature than your first image

is negative. In other words, the intense feelings generated by your positive image are more intense than the negative ones generated by the negative image.

7 Bring this image centre stage and take a good long look at it, noticing its brightness, its vibrancy and its warmth.

8 Now take this image and push it away – as it moves into the distance shrink it, make the colour drain out and the sound diminish, until it looks like a small grey postage stamp.

9 Bring back the original negative image in front of you and place the small grey postage stamp in the bottom right-hand corner.

10 On the count of three, make the two images change places. The negative image will collapse and the positive one will 'swish' all over it becoming bright and powerful.

11 Repeat steps 9–11 as many times as it takes for you to find it difficult to bring back the original image. The positive one will just want to appear instead.

Successful sales people:

■ ask great questions to gain clarity around their prospects' thinking;

■ use this information to focus their sales pitch on providing a solution;

■ resist the temptation to be defensive;

■ keep a check on negative thinking – using techniques to change their thinking from limiting to productive.

06

What are you aiming for?

Knowing precisely what you want from your career, your prospects and clients, your telephone calls and your meetings can save you a great deal of time, as well as keep you focused. In this chapter you will learn how to set well-formed outcomes for the things you do within your role in sales.

Tom's story

Tom is never disappointed when he goes out on a sales call. In fact his day's work is never disappointing. His role is to persuade local and national businesses to work towards greener business practices by increasing the percentage of products they recycle, changing their fuel usage and reducing their carbon emissions. Tom knows that clients do not make changes of this kind overnight – change comes in well-planned stages, so he uses well-formed outcomes to set both his own targets and those for his clients. This way, he arrives home every day knowing that he has achieved what he set out to do.

Well-formed outcomes

Most businesspeople have heard of SMART objectives – a system of setting business objectives that fit the criteria of being simple, measurable, achievable, resourced and within a set timescale. NLP offers a wider and deeper, more effective method known as well-formed outcomes. Much angst and frustration in business and indeed in life generally could be eliminated if we set well-formed outcomes for the significant things we do. Setting outcomes for sales targets and for business achievements over a specific period of time is an obvious use of outcome setting, but what about if we had an outcome for attending a meeting, for making a telephone call or for a conversation with a colleague, manager or team member? What would it be like to know exactly what you want out of these activities and to focus on achievement without the extremes of emotion that often accompany them?

So how do we set well-formed outcomes?

Positively stated

Step one is to consider exactly what it is you want from your career, your month's work, your sales meeting or your phone call. State this clearly in the positive: in terms of what you want and not what you don't want. The mind habitually focuses on and is attracted to the things you think about, so if you think about things you want to avoid rather than the things you want to happen then you will be attracted to the very things you wanted to avoid. Consider the statement, 'Whatever you do, please don't think about a red tree.' Of course it's too late, you have to think of the red tree in order to try not to – your mind has been attracted to the red tree, even though I asked you not to think of it.

Example

Mark enjoys free-fall parachuting when he is not working. One afternoon he was sharing a flight with Tina and they were due to land in a field where there was a large open space and a small clump of trees. Before jumping, he heard Tina saying to herself and to others on the flight, 'I must not aim for the trees.' Both before and during her jump her focus was totally on the trees. Guess where she landed – yes, of course, right in the middle of the trees, fortunately without hurting herself.

Those of you who play golf will have had the experience of the ball landing in the bunker or the rough, having focused your internal dialogue so hard on not doing so. If you watch any skilled sports person you will notice that those who win through are not always the ones with extreme technical talent – although of course it goes a long way. The ones with the edge are those who stay focused on what they want to achieve, not on what they do not want to achieve, i.e. the green not the rough. It's the same in business – stating an outcome in the positive, i.e. focusing on what you do want and not on what you don't want, is the first step towards achieving it.

Internal and external resources

Step two is to ensure that you have both the physical and emotional resources. Physical or external resources include equipment, tools, money, people and anything else you may need. External resources may also include skills – sales training, negotiation and influencing skills, listening skills, product knowledge and so on. Internal resources include confidence, courage, clarity of thought, patience, focus, creativity, determination and commitment.

If, after setting your outcome, you find you are lacking one of these internal resources, you can access it from a different scenario. Another presupposition of NLP is:

You have all the resources you need to achieve anything you want.

You just need to be able to transfer resources from one context to another. We can do this by using a technique called anchoring. You are probably unaware that you are anchored to any number of past experiences through your senses, and these anchors trigger different emotions within you. Smells can cause you to remember particular situations and produce either positive or negative feelings, depending on the context. Sounds, such as music, someone's voice, sirens or bird song, can all induce an emotional state in you. Pictures of blue skies and sandy beaches can take you back to that last holiday – and so on.

In a sales environment you may have a poor relationship with a client, for example, and find yourself in a negative state at the very sound of their voice. Such a state is unlikely to produce a positive outcome and you may need to set yourself a more resourceful anchor in order to deal with this client. Here is an exercise to help you.

1 Decide on the internal resource you would like to have in order to achieve this particular outcome – for example, confidence, flexibility or commitment.

2 Recall a time when you had this resource – it can be in a completely different context as long as the feeling matches exactly the resource you are wanting. So, for example, a feeling of confidence may show up as a warm, towering feeling, as if you are being pulled from above, or a feeling of patience may be a warm, cosy feeling that makes you want to breathe deeply and calmly and smile.

3 Focus your gaze above the horizon and on the picture created by your memory. Increase the intensity of the colour in the picture, and make sure you can see every detail, hear the sounds and experience the emotions of the occasion.

4 When you have the picture as clear as possible, bring it forward and, as you do so, make it bigger and brighter until it is close enough for you to mentally step into it.

5 Notice the feelings you are experiencing at this moment and exaggerate them – imagine they are moving and speed them up or slow them down as is most appropriate.

6 Now – set an anchor. You can choose either a physical anchor such as squeezing your thumb and finger together or linking your hands in a specific way, or an auditory anchor such as a few bars of a memorable song. If you prefer, you can set a visual anchor of a picture you can recall that represents this feeling for you. Physical anchors work well because they are easily accessible any time and anywhere. As the feeling peaks, set your anchor and hold on to it until the feeling begins to dissipate and then let go.

7 You can test your anchor by firing it again after a few moments' break – if the positive feelings return then it has worked. Practise using your anchor just before any scenario

where you think you might need this particular resource. Eventually you will find that you have reprogrammed yourself and won't need to use your anchor again.

8 You can set anchors to access several different resources, but make sure that you choose different physical anchors so that you don't inadvertently fire the wrong one at the wrong time. For example, you may choose pressing your first finger and thumb of your right hand together for confidence and on your left hand for patience.

The secret of success for this exercise is in the precision with which you set the anchor and the intensity of the feelings associated with the resource you require. Practise several times, and then when you need this resource simply fire your anchor and the resource will return. Eventually you won't need the anchor, as your mind gets the message that you want this resource and learns exactly how to access it.

Initiated and maintained by self

Step three of your outcome setting process is to ensure that your outcome is initiated and maintained by you. You may, of course, need other people to help you to achieve your outcome, but an outcome that depends on external factors that are out of your control is not well formed and not within your sphere of influence.

Example

Daniel sold tinfoil food containers to the restaurant industry. He often made promises to his clients that his production team could not fulfil. Consequently, his clients were often disappointed by late deliveries and shortfalls in their orders. They learnt not to trust him and soon Daniel found himself losing customers. Had Daniel taken the trouble to build strong relationships with the production team, he would have been able to ensure that his outcomes were well formed and make promises to his clients that he could keep.

Ecology check

Step four is to check that your outcome is ecologically sound. What will happen if you achieve this outcome? How will it affect your prospect, your client, your company, your team, your family and you? If the consequences have a negative impact on anyone or anything, is this acceptable? If so, then how are you going to deal with the consequences? Not all outcomes can have totally positive impacts. For example, if you have to change the delivery schedule for your client, how is this going to affect your production and logistics teams? Can you accept responsibility for being able to influence them to make the changes?

Sensory-based evidence

Step five is to step back and enjoy having achieved your goal. Yes, I mean already having achieved it. Imagine having achieved it and checking with your senses what it feels like to have done all the things you did to get there. Create a very clear picture of what you can see, hear and feel as a result of achieving your outcome. Remember to make it big, colourful and clear – bring it forward and mentally step into the picture. This process will not only give you an opportunity to enjoy your achievement, it will also allow you to identify things you may have missed in the planning.

Timescale

The last step is to put a timescale on your outcome. When will you have completed it?

Achieving well-formed outcomes

In summary, here is a mnemonic to help you remember the criteria for well-formed outcomes:

P is for positively stated.

R is for internal and external resources.

I is for initiated and maintained by self.

E is for ecology check.

S is for sensory-based evidence.

T is for timescale.

Clarifying and integrating well-formed outcomes

Here is an exercise to help you to integrate medium- and long-term outcomes. You may find this useful for setting team challenges and targets, as well as for setting your own sales outcomes.

1 Put a marker on the floor to represent now.

2 Walk forward in a straight line to a point that represents a time when you will have achieved your outcome.

3 Place something that represents your well-formed outcome on the floor at this point. This could be an object or a piece of card with a symbol on it or even the outcome written simply, clearly and positively.

4 Stand behind this point, looking back to the marker representing 'now'.

5 Take a few minutes to enjoy having achieved your outcome. Enjoy what you can see, feel and hear.

6 Ask yourself what you did first in order to achieve this outcome. Be precise and do not be tempted to skip anything. Then ask yourself what you did next and then after that, until you have completed your step-by-step plan.

7 Write it down while it is still fresh in your mind.

Returning to our earlier story, Tom makes a point of following this process in all areas of his role. At the beginning of every sales period he gets his team together in a room with lots of space. Between them they agree their targets for each period and use this timeline exercise to establish their joint and individual plans. The team leaves the meeting with their own clear objectives, as well as a full understanding of those of each other member of the team. Tom also uses the well-formed outcome structure to establish his outcomes for each sales meeting. He knows that each of his customers will make differing levels of commitment to his green products and he sets outcomes that will allow them to make the changes step by step. He knows that there can be more than one outcome for each meeting and checks each of these for well-formedness before visiting his clients. In this way Tom sets himself and his team up for success and, as far as humanly possible, eliminates unpleasant surprises.

Setting outcomes at the sales meeting

A great way to ensure success at the beginning of a sales meeting, or any meeting for that matter, is for everyone to agree their outcomes. As the leader in the sales process, it is up to you to clarify the outcomes for those present. Some specific questions for your prospect will be:

- What would you like to see at the end of this meeting?
- How far would you like to get today?
- How long do we have?
- Are you OK with a PowerPoint presentation? (State the time length and purpose.)
- All things being equal, when do you see yourself beginning to use this product?

Setting clear outcomes at the outset puts everyone in the position of knowing what to expect and where you expect to be by the end of the process.

Successful sales people:

- set well-formed outcomes for themselves;
- begin every sales meeting by setting outcomes;
- help their teams to set their own well-formed outcomes;
- ensure they have everything they need in order to achieve their outcomes including internal and external resources;
- anchor resourceful states for selling.

07

Rapport gets you everywhere

In order to benefit from all that you have learnt so far you will need to learn how to build rapport. Having the best products in the world and all the sales techniques to go with them will get you nowhere without rapport. I am sure you have had the experience of wanting to buy something but were put off by a disinterested or seemingly arrogant sales person. Quite simply, people generally buy from people they get on with and can trust. In this chapter you will learn to build strong rapport before beginning the process of pacing and leading your prospects and clients to a successful sale.

Sam's story

Sam sells pharmaceutical products to hospitals. He knows that to be able to introduce new product lines he has to demonstrate them to the people who will be using them, i.e. the nurses. Nurses are, of course, busy people and pinning them down to appointment times is a challenge. Sam also knows that if the nurses like his product they will request them via the buying team, and repeat orders will become part of the computerised buying system. Sam takes time and care to build rapport with the nurses before ever trying to sell them anything. He arrives at the hospital prepared to wait until they are free. He takes paperwork with him and keeps himself busy while he is waiting. This is an important part of his strategy to make the nurses feel they are not keeping him waiting. When they stop for a break, he will fetch or even make the tea and coffee for them and listen to their accounts of what it is like being a nurse in a busy hospital. When the time is right, he keeps his product demonstrations short and leaves samples for the nurses to try out when an opportunity presents itself. He never demonstrates more than two products at a time. Very quickly Sam's products become part of the product availability listing for the hospitals and his sales soar.

Compare this approach to sharp-suited Eric, who fills his day with appointments and becomes frustrated when he cannot get to see the nurses within his carefully planned time schedule. He invariably has to leave for his next appointment without seeing anyone, and has to make a new appointment for later – and so the pattern repeats itself.

Rapport is everything in building relationships

At a recent presentation the delegates were asked to list their pet hates in relation to sales approaches. Their top hates (though not necessarily in this order) were sales people who:

- stick to their script, regardless of the contribution you make;
- don't listen;
- make assumptions about you and your needs;
- are dishonest about their intentions – for example, they start their approach with 'We are doing some research into ...' or 'You have won a competition';
- invade your privacy – for example, calling during the evening or asking personal questions;
- refuse to give you the price, regardless of how many times you ask, until they have finished what they want to say;
- record their messages and dial telephone numbers randomly;
- don't take no for an answer and keep calling back;
- are insincere in their friendly approach – unfounded flattery;
- become familiar too quickly and make inappropriate jokes/ inferences;
- claim the product – for example, a car or house – was once owned by a friend, colleague or relative, as if this makes it desirable.

It's not surprising that people find these approaches irritating at the very least. These approaches all have one thing in common – they lack rapport. Without rapport, it does not matter how effective and competitively priced your product is, people will resist buying from you.

Test this for yourself – think about the last few serious purchases you made, other than those you made on the internet. What was it about the sales person that helped you make your decision?

Have you ever bought something from someone you did not have any rapport with? Have you ever bought something just because you had rapport and you did not want to let the sales person down, or they made you laugh?

Sam built his approach by putting himself in the shoes of the nurses. He also knew that it was the nurses who would have the final say about his products, not the buying teams. So he set about devising a strategy based on building rapport with the nurses. He asked himself:

- What is it like to be a nurse in a busy hospital?
- If I was up to my ears in patient care, how would I feel about a smart-suited sales person appearing with a briefcase full of new products and brochures?
- What can I do to make their lives easier and help them to make a decision?
- How can I fit in with their timescales?
- How can I make sure that they are comfortable having me around the hospital?

By understanding what it was like to be a nurse in a busy hospital, Sam was able to identify with them and present his products in a way that was acceptable to them.

Putting yourself in your prospects' and clients' shoes

Before you go to your next appointment, try this. Imagine you are in the room where you will have your next important sales meeting. Imagine what it will look like and where people might be sitting or standing. You are now going to view this scenario from three different viewpoints and gain some awareness from each of them that you can take to your meeting.

Viewpoint 1

From your own position, answer the following questions:

- What exactly do I want to get out of the meeting?
- What do I believe about the people I am meeting?
- What do I know or believe about the organisation or industry I am dealing with here?
- What impact are my metaprogrammes, values and beliefs likely to have on the sales process?
- What is important to me about this meeting?
- How well prepared am I?
- What else can I do to make it easy for this prospect to buy from me?

Viewpoint 2

Now imagine that you are your prospect or your customer looking at and listening to you, and ask yourself the following questions from their viewpoint:

- How is this sales person [you] behaving?
- Do they know their stuff?
- Are they sincere? Do they really believe what they are saying?
- Do they look confident or are they nervous?
- Are they boring me rigid with detail or are they not giving me enough?
- Are they listening to me?
- Do they understand what is needed here?
- Do they really appreciate my position?
- What is important to them?
- Are they trying to help me or are they only interested in achieving a sale?

- What does their body posturing suggest?
- What do I [the prospect or client] want from this meeting?
- What is important to me [the prospect or client]?
- What do I [the prospect or client] believe about this meeting/ this person/our ability to buy/our readiness for change?
- What do I [the prospect or client] believe about sales people generally?

Of course you will have to take an educated guess at the answers to these last few questions. If negative beliefs begin to surface, remember they may be your own personal beliefs based on conclusions you have come to from previous experiences. Refer back to the section on dealing with negative beliefs in Chapter 5 if you need to.

Viewpoint 3

Now imagine you are a fly on the wall where you can see both you and your prospect or client clearly. From this position ask yourself:

- What can I learn from this observation that will help me in my meeting?
- What can I do differently to get a positive result for both of us?
- Am I congruent with what I am doing and saying?
- What else can I do to help this person buy from me?

Building rapport

Now that you have gained an insight into what it is like to be your prospect and what they expect from you and your sales meeting, it is time to prepare yourself thoroughly for the real experience. By now you will have done your homework and have discovered as much as you can about your prospect, their needs and their company. You will also have established that the person you are about to visit has the power to buy – in other words, you are talking with the right person or people. You will have prepared a presentation and gathered your materials and samples. If you have already spoken on the telephone or via e-mail to your prospect, you will already have begun the rapport-building process, so let's take a look at what excellent sales people do to build rapport.

What is rapport and why is it important?

You can have the best product or service in the world but if you fail to build rapport with your clients your sales will suffer seriously. Remember that 'people buy people'. We have already discussed in this book a number of examples where buyers have made decisions based on whether or not the sales person appeals to them. People rarely buy things from people they do not feel some kind of empathy with. There are a number of things you can do to help build rapport with people, particularly if they are people you do not initially feel a natural leaning towards.

Example

Tim and Suzi recently decided to replace their en suite shower room furniture. Having explored a few possibilities, Suzi popped into a reputable store, looked around the showroom and collected some catalogues. Some time later the company called to see if they could send out a designer – Tim and Suzi happily agreed. On the day of the call the company called again to say that the designer they had intended to send had phoned in sick and would they mind if someone else came instead. Not knowing either of the designers, Suzi and Tim again happily agreed.

Graham, the sales representative, arrived and made a number of basic mistakes:

- He smelled of stale tobacco.

- He did not set an expectation for the duration of his visit.

- He failed to notice Suzi's look of horror when he proceeded to set up a large screen and a laptop on the kitchen table. Suzi spends all day looking at a computer screen and the last thing she wanted to do in the evening was to spend a couple of hours in front of another one – after all, the en suite shower room consisted of a toilet, a shower and a vanity unit – how much designing did it need? These feelings were exacerbated by Graham's slow speed of operation and the fact that the design program failed to work on a number of occasions.

- He referred to Suzi as 'the boss' in a cynical manner.

- He mentioned that some of the items were on 50 per cent offer but failed to say which ones, so that by the time the design process was complete he appeared to take pleasure in telling Tim and Suzi that they had chosen a very expensive suite. At this stage they were in no mood to start the whole process again and so Graham left after two hours with no sale.

- He failed to recognise the role of the computerised design system. A bit like a PowerPoint presentation, such a system is a support for the process. Once you allow the system to take over, you lose control of the engagement or rapport-building process.

A few rapport-building techniques could have saved Graham a great deal of trouble. He didn't need to use his computerised design service – Suzi and Tim knew what they wanted and knew how much money they wanted to spend, so with a few measurements and a few pictures he could have been away in 30 minutes and on to his next prospect.

Simply put, rapport is the process of getting on well together. There are some people – your friends, for example – with whom you will naturally have rapport and be able to pick up quickly from where you left off when you were last in touch. There will be people you come across in your sales role who you will be drawn to and with whom you will quickly build a relationship. It's generally these relationships that bring fast results because there appears to be mutual understanding. It is this type of understanding that you can replicate with all your clients – not just the ones with whom you have natural rapport.

To really understand what rapport is, try watching people from a distance to see what you notice. Here are some examples:

- Two people chatting in a restaurant – what tells you they are friends, lovers, business associates or maybe have been married a long time?
- Someone making a complaint in a shop – is the conversation amicable or hostile?
- Two men standing at the bar in your local pub – what happens when they laugh? Do they drink at the same time? What is their body posturing doing?
- People chatting at a party.

Matching and mirroring

Rapport building is a process of matching and mirroring people elegantly and with integrity. By this I mean either matching some of the things listed below, or doing the opposite, i.e. mirroring. It is a natural process and one that can be used consciously to build strong relationships. Here are some things to look out for where you can match and mirror:

- **Body positioning**: People with strong rapport generally mirror or match each other's body positions and movements. If one person is sitting forward, the other generally does the same. The legs will be crossed at the same or similar angle, the head tilted the same way – look out for the hands, the shoulders and even the breathing. This is not a conscious process; it is something that happens as two people begin to move towards each other and create an unwritten understanding.

■ **Body movement**: Watch what happens when one person moves or laughs or makes some kind of expression. If one person throws their head back in laughter then, if rapport is strong, the other will follow. If one takes a deep breath and displays an expression of disgust, shock, horror, passion, love, sentiment, curiosity or general satisfaction then, again, if rapport is strong, the other person will emulate it. Learn to pace and lead people by following body movements.

What else goes into building rapport?

If you can get close enough to people in rapport you will notice they have a lot more in common than just their body movements. Here are some more things that go into creating strong rapport between people and that can be used in the rapport-building process.

Values and beliefs

Shared values are a strong rapport builder. As a sales person, find out what is important to your prospect – even if you don't share the same values, then at least empathise with and respect theirs. Earlier I mentioned the NLP presupposition:

Respect other people's maps of the world.

If everyone is different and we all have different perceptions of reality, then no one person is in a position to say that one map is right or wrong – just that it's different. In the sales rapport-building process it is vital that we respect other people's maps. Disrespecting someone's map, of which values and beliefs form a large part, can lose you a sale.

Example

Ian overstepped the mark with his client. He thought he had enough rapport with Jerry to tease him about his love of a particular football team and the time Jerry spent following the team's progress. Ian chose the wrong moment to laugh at a particular referee's decision that went against the team. Jerry was offended, believing wholeheartedly that the team had been denied a penalty. The incident became unpleasant and Ian left without a sale. Jerry made the excuse that his budget had been cut and placed his order elsewhere.

Before each meeting, take a moment to think about what is or may be important to your prospect, both in their working role and in their social life. Make sure that throughout your presentation you ask values-based questions:

- What is important to you about xyz product?
- Is it important that it can ...?
- Is it important that the team get to trial it before you buy?
- What are the key features you are looking for here?

You can also use metaprogrammes to pace, lead and build rapport. Refer back to Chapter 2 if you need to. Counting out a process on your fingers or making a list of points will help you to build rapport with someone who values procedures. Recognising important details will help you to build rapport with someone who values specifics, and so on. It is important to recognise that metaprogrammes are a strong part of who we are, and failing to match or acknowledge metaprogrammes can be tantamount to trampling on someone's values.

Also ask some beliefs-based questions:

- What do you believe will happen when you have installed this product?

■ How do you think the team will respond?

■ What do you think will happen if you choose not to buy this product?

Visual, auditory or kinaesthetic processing

Noticing what representation or processing system your prospect is using can be key to your success (see Chapter 3).

Example

Mary and Bob visited Graham, the national training director for a large retail chain. Graham was interested in how to make engagement real for people rather than a tick-box exercise. Graham's office was lined with a number of charts, graphs and pictures of people active in the business. When he took a seat he sat back, often staring out of the window at strategic points of the presentation. Mary and Bob knew this was their cue to be quiet and let Graham visualise and process what had just been presented. Between them they worked on a diagrammatic representation of the solution and Mary and Bob walked away with a significant contract.

Tone, pitch and speed of voice

In Chapter 3 we saw how people with different processing channels are likely to demonstrate differences in their speech. For example, someone who sees moving pictures in their head is likely to speak quickly, breathe from the upper chest and speak in a higher pitch than someone who is using their kinaesthetic channel. By matching the speed, tone and pitch of your prospect's voice, you will be enhancing the rapport-building process. It can be very frustrating to listen to and try to make sense of a fast-speaking sales person who knows their product well but does not have the sensory acuity to slow down to allow others to keep up.

Sense of humour, general outlook and interests

People who share the same sense of humour are likely to get on well, as are those who have the same outlook on life and share the same interests – such as sports, hobbies, academic learning, personal development, places, material things, reading, eating out and films. Remember to use these in the rapport-building process.

Respecting and validating

The key to building rapport successfully is in what you notice about the other person and being able to match it in some way. Successful sales people use their sensory acuity to notice the finer details of people's behaviour. They learn to subtly follow body movement, match voice tone and validate beliefs and values. This does not mean they necessarily agree with them – they just respect and validate.

Use your prospect's focus of attention to build rapport

Have you ever noticed the first thing people say to you when you first meet? It probably covers one of the following areas:

- things
- people
- activities
- locations
- information.

Most people will have a stronger preference for one of these, with a lesser, but still relevant, interest in the others. Learning to spot a prospect's main focus of interest is easy, but without the awareness of how important this is in the rapport-building process you may fail to notice that your prospect has a different focus from your own. Once you become aware, you will be able to use this information right from the beginning of the rapport-building process.

Small talk or big talk?

The conversation built around these areas of interest is sometimes referred to as small talk. I have often heard people say 'I don't do small talk', as though it is a waste of time or unimportant in some way. If this is you, let me offer you a reframe here – let me suggest that this type of opening conversation can lead to contracts being signed, jobs being offered, deals being done, friends being made and strong relationships being established. I would venture to suggest that it is so important that we should call it big talk not small talk. Let's take a look at these areas of interest one at a time.

Things

These people have a strong interest in objects – cars, mobile phones, clothes, shoes, motorbikes, cameras, computers, watches, houses. Their conversation focuses strongly around what's going on in these areas. 'I see you have the latest XY52 supercharge phone, Terry.' 'How do you like your new car?' 'Wearing Burberry again I see.' Their offices often display high-tech gadgets and the latest computers, or they may have specialist paintings or sculptures around the place. They may be collectors of fine arts or antiques, or anything else that appeals to collectors.

When you meet, their first question is likely to be related to some kind of object belonging to you – your car, your watch, your phone or your product samples, or they may tell you about their latest acquisition. This is your cue to validate and show an interest – if you don't, you may be disregarding a fundamental value and inadvertently break rapport.

People

These people will ask about you, your wellbeing, anyone related to you and who you work with. They will concern themselves with the effects buying your products will have on their teams and may need time to gather this information before making a decision. Their offices will often contain photographs of people – family, teams doing things and team members.

Learning to ask about the people that are important to your prospect is key to the rapport-building process here. Remember to record names of people they mention during your meetings so that you can ask about them next time you meet or speak on the telephone.

Activities

'What have you been up to recently?' is a classic question from an activities-focused person. They are interested in what you do, whether it is related to work or your social life. Again, time spent answering this question is time well spent in building strong rapport. Their offices may well be decked with trophies won by company teams or in personal sporting endeavours. You may see a sports bag or even a couple of putters in the corner, or a photograph of their favourite sporting activity on the wall. Beware, sitting listening to a long presentation is not their favourite activity – they would much rather be up and about doing things. Consider taking them for a walk while you discuss your products or services, and keep the period when they have to be sitting to a minimum.

Example

Andy is a business development manager for a young people's charity. His role is to encourage business owners and other wealthy people to part with their money and time in the interests of the charity he represents. Andy is also a Premier League referee and can often be seen on national television refereeing crucial league matches.

Andy finds his activities-focused customers are fascinated by his role on the pitch, whether they follow football or not. His willingness to share his refereeing experiences has gained him much support for his charity.

Locations

Location-focused people are very conscious of their environment. They will pay attention to the location of their office, how it is decorated and what they can see from the window. They are likely to ask you where you have been recently, either with your work or on holiday. You may well have to spend time with these people comparing notes on the locations you have visited. Where you conduct your presentation will also be important to them – make sure that they are comfortable in your chosen environment before you start.

Information

These people's offices may well be lined with books. They are interested in reports, statistics, facts, films, documentaries and/or whatever they can discover on the internet. Their opening gambit may well be, 'What have you got for me?' By this they mean, 'What information can you give me about your products, their success rates, prices and so on?' They may well want validation information, test reports, sales statistics and laboratory reports. Be prepared for this opening.

Satisfying their need for information will help you greatly with building rapport and your ultimate success rate.

Practising rapport-building skills

You will have many opportunities to practise rapport building as you go about your daily life. Try using the techniques in this chapter to build rapport:

- on the telephone;
- with colleagues from other parts of your organisation;
- with the waiter or sandwich-bar owner when buying your lunch;
- when enquiring about a new product you would like to buy;
- when meeting new people at the gym or tennis club;
- in the taxi queue or the queue for the post office or airport security.

See what you can find out about people – you will be amazed at what they will tell you once you have built their trust.

Pacing and leading using the link anything to anything technique

Having built rapport with your prospect using the techniques described, it is time to begin your presentation. Remember that rapport needs to be maintained throughout and you may need some techniques to get back on track if your prospect sidetracks, goes off at a tangent or becomes distracted in some way. The link anything to anything technique is based on the metaprogramme global/detail and works on the basis that we communicate in different chunk sizes. Here is a simple example of what I mean by chunk sizes:

- Human innovation (global level 1)
- Technology (level 2)
- Office equipment (level 3)
- *Computer (level 4) – desk – photocopier – chair – filing cabinet*

- Laptop (level 5)
- Acer brand (level 6)
- My laptop! (detail level 7)

From the word computer I can chunk up through the various levels to human innovation or I can chunk down through the various levels to talk about the particular laptop computer I use. I could equally chunk sideways from computer to other examples of office equipment, such as desk, photocopier, chair and filing cabinet. There are two simple questions that determine the chunking levels:

- To chunk up the question is, 'What is a computer an example of?'
- To chunk down the question is, 'What is an example of a computer?'

'So what?' I hear you say. Imagine being engaged in a conversation about technology with your supermarket buyer prospect, perhaps because she has just had a new laptop delivered and is struggling to get all the programs she needs installed. She is unloading her frustration on you as you arrive for your sales meeting. You can use this link anything to anything technique to get her focused on your presentation about a new brand of dog food your company has just introduced – smoothly and elegantly.

Here is how it might go:

Prospect: I've just been trying to download xyz program on to my new super-duper, flash, do-everything laptop but I can't seem to get it to work. Don't you just hate technology? [She has chunked from one specific laptop right up to technology in general.]

You: [join her at the level of technology] We'd be lost without it though – think of all the great things you did with your last laptop and all the computerised buying mechanisms you have in your stores. It would be awful if you had to go back to physically counting the stock on a daily basis and placing paper orders for every product in the store, wouldn't it?

Prospect: Yes, you're right, of course that would be very time consuming – I shudder to think of it.

You: Talking of stock levels, I noticed as I came through the store that you haven't got our new product on display.

You can join any conversation and pace and lead people to where you want to be elegantly and quickly using this technique. Practise – it's fun!

The importance of rapport

There is an NLP presupposition relating to rapport:

Resistance is a sign of a lack of rapport!

If you have ever been in a situation where rapport is lacking, you will recall the resistance you felt at the time. Whether this was with someone trying to sell you something or maybe trying to get to know you in a social setting, if rapport was absent then a positive result was unlikely. It is only when you take the trouble to build rapport that people begin to warm towards you and you can begin to pace and lead them.

Successful sales people:

■ metaphorically step into their prospects' and clients' shoes to gain more information that will help them to buy;

■ practise their rapport-building skills;

- identify their prospect's focus of interest and work with it to build rapport;
- make sure they are speaking to the decision maker;
- demonstrate flexibility by adjusting their approach for different prospects and clients;
- use the link anything to anything technique to elegantly pace and lead;
- know the value of big talk;
- know that without rapport a sale is unlikely.

08

The elegant language of sales

Successful sales people learn to use elegant language structures designed to elegantly pace and lead their prospects towards a sale. Here you will learn how to use these structures and to use an anchoring technique to anchor positive buying states in your clients and prospects.

Trevor's story

Trevor has learned to use a combination of anchors and language patterns to encourage his clients to buy from him. He does this both to achieve the sale and to help his more indecisive prospects to make a decision on something over which they may normally procrastinate. He changes his tone of voice whenever he wants his prospect to do something – for example, to look at the brochure or try out a sample. The prospect gets used to responding positively to the change in Trevor's voice so that when it comes to asking for the sale, by changing the tone of his voice, he gets a positive response from his prospect.

A step-by-step approach

In this chapter I am going to show you how to use anchoring and language patterns to pace and lead your prospect to a sale. This technique keeps your prospect focused and allows you to keep control of the sales process. Remember that you are not misleading your prospect – they are unlikely to buy something they do not want and need, whatever techniques you use. You are simply making it easy for your prospect to become a customer. First, I will describe the two techniques separately.

Anchoring

In Chapter 6 you learnt how to anchor resourceful states for yourself so that you can quickly call on resources such as confidence, patience, understanding, being a good listener and so on. Anchoring is something that happens naturally – we become anchored to smells, images, feelings, tastes and sounds. For example, if you hear a tune that was playing at a particularly significant moment in your life you will be instantly transported back to the incident in your mind. Certain smells will remind you of certain places – dentists' surgeries and school dining rooms, for example, both have their own particular smell and you can quickly be transported back to the last time you experienced either of these when you smell something similar. If you touch something soft and fluffy, you will probably associate it with something else that is familiar to you – maybe your cat or dog or a favourite sweater. It is a simple, stimulus-response reaction.

This type of anchoring is automatic and in some ways haphazard. Without the awareness that it is happening it appears to be out of your control. It is possible, however, to use anchoring in a positive, proactive way in order to help your prospect buy from you. The first thing to remember is that sometimes people become negatively anchored to an environment, so make sure that if possible you arrange your sales meeting in a place that is free from such anchors. For example, if the last time you visited the client you had a particularly sticky time, try to sit somewhere different so that your client has to position themselves differently. If appropriate, you could go for a coffee or take a walk in the park – be creative, thinking of ways to break unproductive anchors. If your client always sees sales people in the same room, use your sensory acuity to assess whether the client is positively or negatively anchored to this environment.

Example

Dominic sells garden furniture. Having made an appointment to demonstrate his new range of products to the board of a national company, he was disappointed to arrive and find the key decision maker had been called away at short notice. Dominic also knew from previous experience of the company that the decision maker always sat in the same chair and that it was unlikely that a decision would be made without him. He began his presentation, which was very well received, and then when the time came to ask for the sale he moved slowly around the table and stood behind the empty chair, leaning on the back support. All heads had to turn in order to look at him – the group was now in its anchored decision-making position, looking at the place where the main decision maker normally sat. Dominic left the meeting with an order.

You can anchor positive decision-making states in your client. Use your sensory acuity to notice when a client is in a state that is useful to the process. They could be nodding agreement, laughing light-heartedly or listening intently. You may want to anchor the state they display when asked to do something such as look at a brochure, handle the products or watch a video clip, so that you can bring them back to this state when you ask them a question that requires them to do something later on – make a decision, for example. Once you have noticed the state you are looking for, you will see it repeated at various times throughout your presentation. Each time it appears, anchor it by using one of the following:

- Change your tone of voice.
- Slow your speech right down, emphasising each word.
- Tap a pen or brochure lightly.
- Point your finger upwards.

■ Make a particular movement.

■ Something else you have found to work.

Choose your anchor carefully, taking into account the processing preferences your client displays. For example, if your client shows a preference for auditory processing, tapping may be irritating to them. Make it subtle and keep it congruent. When you are ready to use your anchor to encourage a decision, do so elegantly – you may even decide to test it first on something small. For example, before asking for the sale, you could ask for a decision about something less significant and monitor your client's response.

Language patterns to pace and lead

In Chapter 5 you learnt how to identify language patterns that indicated the presence of a limiting belief and to ask appropriate questions to shake and replace the belief. This section will focus on using language patterns to elegantly pace and lead your prospect towards a sale. The patterns were first used in therapeutic hypnosis by Milton Erickson to help his clients move to more positive mindsets. The patterns are often referred to as Miltonian patterns, or artfully vague language. The intention here is not to 'fool' your prospect into making a decision, but to make it easy for them to do so having used your integrity and sensory acuity to ensure that this is the right course of action for them to take. You are using your language skills to:

■ keep your customer focused and on track;

■ prevent distractions;

■ reinforce positive ideas and contributions;

■ assure congruent behaviour in relation to values and beliefs of both you and your prospect;

- clear away objections and queries to ensure that a win/win decision is made;
- maintain rapport;
- demonstrate understanding, creativity and your genuine desire for a solution.

Embedded suggestion

The key to using an embedded suggestion is to be clear about what exactly you want your prospect to do next and then embed the suggestion into your conversation or presentation. Here are some examples:

- *When you use this product in your organisation*, you will find that it offers exceptional quality for three reasons …
- You will benefit from all the features, *just as soon as the agreement is signed.*
- *Having installed this new system*, you will find that it gives you all the features you have been looking for.

Presuppositions

A presupposition presupposes that something has either taken place, been in existence or is going to happen. You can use it to help your prospect to become aware of something they had not really considered, were ignoring or were procrastinating over. For example:

- *When you take training off the backburner* and begin to look towards developing your management team, you will realise just how powerful these techniques can be. [This statement presupposes that training has been on the backburner and gives you an opportunity to bring it into the open for discussion.]
- *Another advantage of using NLP* to train your sales teams is that NLP offers fast, effective techniques for changing

non-productive behaviours into productive behaviours, and this will directly impact your bottom line. [This statement presupposes that there are other advantages of using NLP, which either have been discussed previously or are up for discussion in the future.]

- *One of the ways* our company can help you to solve this challenge is to … [This statement presupposes that there are other ways if this one does not suit.]

- *When you simplify your training matrix*, you will find measuring key performance indicators a much more rewarding and productive exercise for all involved. [This statement presupposes that the training matrix is currently complex and that it will be simplified.]

- *Whichever product you choose*, you will have the peace of mind of a full guarantee. [This statement presupposes your prospect will choose a product.]

Tag questions

A tag question is a short question asked at the end of a statement to gain agreement. The intention is to pace and lead your prospect with things that you have already established they agree with. You are making it easy for your prospect to buy from you. The more you can gain agreement throughout your presentation, the more likely you are to achieve a sale. For example:

- It makes sense to ensure that your management team is as skilled in these techniques as possible, *doesn't it*?

- Being able to increase your sphere of influence with your customers is going to pay dividends, *isn't it*?

- You would rather stay ahead of the competition with a highly skilled sales team, *wouldn't you*?

- Your managing director would be very impressed if you pulled in this huge contract, *wouldn't they*?

- Getting these new concepts into the organisation sooner rather than later would make good sense, *wouldn't it*?
- You are the budget holder for this particular project, *aren't you*?
- You do have a well-thought-through plan for this project after all, *don't you*?
- You would sooner be making a profit this year than next, *wouldn't you*?

Think about the response you are looking for when using a tag question: if you want an answer, raise the tone of your voice when you come to the tag question; if you are reinforcing something that is true in order to focus your prospect and get a decision, then lower the tone of your voice.

Phonological ambiguity

There are a number of words in the English language that sound the same but have different meanings identifiable by their spelling and the context in which they are used. Some examples include:

- buy and by and bi
- slay and sleigh
- bear and bare
- draw and drawer
- fore and four and for
- eight and ate
- know and no
- to and two and too.

If you have reached the stage of your presentation where your prospect is ready to buy but just needs a little help, you can make elegant suggestions by using phonological ambiguity. The unconscious mind does not hear the spelling, simply the sound of the word. For example:

- *Buy now* you will have all the information you need in order to make a decision and will probably be wondering about the timescales we can offer you for the installation.

Linking anchors to language

At the beginning of this chapter you learnt how to anchor positive states in your prospect. When you are ready to agree the sale, you can regenerate this state in your client in preparation for buying by firing your anchor. Make no mistake, your clients won't do something they are unwilling to do when you use this technique – and if, by any chance, they do then this will be the first and last time they buy from you. The technique is simply to create a productive, agreeable, buying environment where your clients can feel comfortable with the decision they have made.

Using your prospect's metaphors

In Chapter 3 we saw how people with different processing systems use different linguistic metaphors to describe their experiences. You can use these metaphors to pace and lead your prospect. Listen for language structures that you can use to develop the metaphor later in the conversation. Here are some examples of some commonly used metaphors and some ways you can develop them:

- *Singing from the same hymn sheet.* If we could include some different notes on the hymn sheet in the form of xyz products, how would that sound?

- *Take a long-term view.* If we were to take a similar view from the other side, having put xyz product in place, what would you see?

- *Bird's eye view.* Let's fly up and take that view again, now that we have rearranged the landscape slightly.

- *See it through their eyes.* If you were to take another look through their eyes, can you see the benefits of taking this course of action?

- *Take a different angle.* Let's look at yet another angle to this.

- *Give me a few sound bites.* Sound bite 1 will be to take course A, sound bite 2 will be to take course B, and then you have the option to take sound bite C.

- *I'll have the one with all the bells and whistles.* So if we include the deluxe leather upholstery, the top-of-the-range audio system and the state-of-the-art navigation system, does that sound like all the bells and whistles?

- *It screams out for some more colour.* What else can you hear it screaming for?

- *Rock hard.* Our agreement will, of course, be settled on some rock-hard principles.

- *Getting round barriers.* So if we get round this barrier, will this give you a straight track?

- *Jumping through hoops.* When you have jumped through this hoop, is there a soft landing on the other side?

- *It's like walking through treacle.* Let's see if we can at least thin the treacle to make it an easier passage.

- *Joining up the dots.* If all the dots were joined, what sort of a picture would they make?

- *Push the boat out.* If you were to push the boat out, what would the view be like from outside the harbour?

- *It's like spinning plates.* If you could keep all the plates in the air at once, what would that feel like?

Using metaphors in this way will give the prospect the impression that you are really listening to and understanding their needs and viewpoint. Practise listening for metaphors and see how many you can use in this way.

Third-party evidence

Third-party evidence can be very useful in backing up your presentation, particularly if you sense your prospect is externally referenced. Practise delivering third-party evidence in the form of an informal quote. For example, 'When I called Mr Blip yesterday he told me that he was over the moon with xyz product because he could leave it running in the background and he had more time to spend serving his customers.'

Be careful not to use this technique with people who are internally referenced because they really will not care what other people think of your products, preferring to use their own judgement and make up their own mind.

Successful sales people:

- use anchors to create positive buying states in their clients;
- use elegant language structures to pace and lead their prospects;
- help their prospects to make decisions by keeping them focused;
- develop their prospect's metaphors in the pacing and leading process;
- test for congruency before asking for the sale.

09

Using frames to keep control

You will want to maintain control of the sales process and work towards your well-formed outcome during your sales activities. Frames are a way of structuring a meeting and keeping it on track while encouraging flexible discussion.

Paul's story

The technical and wide-ranging nature of the products Paul sold often resulted in his clients becoming fascinated by the benefits of a product for which they had no use. Paul would spend a great deal of time satisfying their curiosity, knowing full well that this was not going to result in a sale. He would leave the meeting frustrated because he had not managed to keep his clients on track. Consequently his sales figures suffered and increasingly he began to miss his targets. Paradoxically, the more Paul learnt about his products, the worse the problem became. Then he discovered frames.

What are frames?

Frames are an excellent way of keeping a sales meeting on track. Think of frames as a means of putting a boundary around each section of your presentation or discussion – a bit like the triangle you place around the red balls on a snooker table to stop them escaping at the beginning of a game. You can move the frames around, return to them when you want them, add new ones and develop existing ones, but the intention is to keep your discussion on track and not allow your customer or prospect to sidetrack you inappropriately.

Let's take a look at the frames that are most useful for sales and suggest some ways you can use them. You don't, of course, need to use them all – select the ones that are most appropriate for any given situation.

Outcome frame

In Chapter 6 we looked at the value of setting well-formed outcomes. By using the outcome frame effectively, you can find out exactly what it is that your prospective client wants to get from your meeting. Use the questioning technique you learnt in Chapter 5 to:

- discover specific client needs;
- set timescales for the meeting;
- explore budgetary parameters;
- explore product delivery requirements.

Then use this information to:

- mentally delete anything from your presentation that is going to cause a distraction or diversion – for example, the functions of a product that your prospect is unlikely to use;
- make mental notes to emphasise important sections of your presentation.

If you have to help your prospect to clarify their outcomes, continue to ask questions elegantly. Only move out of this frame when you are clear about your prospect's outcomes and have made mental adjustments to your own.

You can also link this frame to the alignment model (see Chapter 4). Find out what purpose your prospect has for researching your products or services. It may be that you can fulfil this purpose in another way. For example, we often get asked for training programmes to service a need that could be satisfied better with one-to-one coaching or attendance on one of our open programmes, and vice versa.

Backtrack frame

If you have met with the client previously or had any communication with them before the meeting, it can sometimes be useful to backtrack just in case anything has changed. Simply summarise your assessment of where you are, at a high level, and ask if your prospect agrees that this is accurate. You can also ask if they want to add anything at this stage: if things have changed, it should come to light here. Notice the careful use of the words 'add anything' rather than 'change'. You want to keep the meeting moving forward and 'add anything' has a progressive tone to it.

You can also use this frame at any stage during the meeting to recap on what you have agreed and what still needs discussion.

Ecology frame

Sometimes your prospects do not think about the impact that their purchase might have on people around them. Use this frame to check the impact of achieving your prospect's outcomes on any of the following that are relevant:

- their teams
- their customers
- their families
- the environment
- other parts of the business
- other products in the range
- employment levels
- productivity levels
- training requirements.

If changing over to your product requires a 'bedding-in' period while everyone is trained, then this is the frame in which to highlight this. Explain that productivity may be a bit bumpy for a while, and reassure your client that once everything beds down, productivity will surpass previous levels. Reassure them also that you will be with them all the way during the bedding-in period.

Keep in mind your knowledge of metaprogrammes here. For example, someone whose focus of interest is people will have already considered the implications for the team, employment issues and anything else related to people. In fact, this concern may be so strong that you may have to work hard to convince your prospect that people will not suffer through the introduction of your products. Someone who is things focused may believe that having the latest equipment is the way to motivate people, and so on.

The ecology frame is also an opportunity for you to reassess your own integrity in the light of new information or information that you have but have not revealed to your prospect. Ask yourself, 'If I complete this sale, will I be happy that this really is the best solution for this particular client?'

'Act as if' frame

This frame is an opportunity for you to control thinking around various alternative solutions that your prospect might be considering. For example, 'Let's just suppose for a moment that you select product A, you will be able to instantly solve challenges 1 and 2, but challenge 3 will need another solution. Let's take a few minutes to explore the implications and consequences of this.' You can then move on to another scenario, keeping it clear that you are only considering one solution at a time by putting the 'act as if' frame around each one.

This frame is particularly good for helping people to become unstuck, because it can temporarily remove any perceived objections. So you can 'act as if':

- you have got the budget;
- you have approval from the budget holder;
- you can overcome specific objections;
- you can overcome location issues;
- you have the right people in the right places;
- you can find employment for anyone who is displaced as a result of installing your products;
- everyone is trained and ready to go;
- delivery times are acceptable.

By working through the scenarios and exciting your client about the positive benefits your product or service can offer, the objections can often appear smaller and very much more surmountable.

Contrast frame

Use this frame to compare and contrast the benefits of products or services within your range, or with your competitors' products. For example, 'Let's compare these two products – if you opt for product A then you will receive benefits 1, 2 and 3. If you opt for product B then you will have benefits 1 and 2, but you may struggle with 3.'

Only use this frame if you sense that your prospect is making this comparison. They may not be considering your competitors' products, so if you introduce this frame you may be suggesting a new idea for them.

Evidence frame

This frame has a number of uses. For example, if you sense that your prospect is particularly externally referenced, you may spend some time in this frame producing evidence of the effectiveness of your products in terms of testimonials, reports and data from external sources. Alternatively, if you sense your prospect has acquired some unreliable data and is showing some resistance as a result, you may spend some time in this frame exploring the source of their data and gently shaking the associated limiting beliefs.

Discovery frame

This frame can be used to open the discussion up a little and explore new ideas. However, use it with caution because you can sometimes open minefields, as well as offer an opportunity for distraction and diversion, which may or may not be useful. So keep control of the frame by introducing it with something like, 'Let's take 10 minutes here to discover what else we might need in order to finalise a solution.' At the end of the 10 minutes, summarise and decide whether you need more time or whether it is time to exit – either for you or for your client to gather more information. If you decide to exit, make sure you set another date to regroup and be clear about what new information is needed in order for you all to proceed.

Relevancy frame

Sometimes your prospects will get stuck – for example, they may be attracted by a feature of your product which could be of use elsewhere in the organisation, or be looking at something that is intriguing but not relevant to the sale. These are your cues to decide whether or not to put the relevancy frame into operation.

- Your response to the first example might be: 'That's an excellent idea – why don't we set aside some time to give it the space it deserves? I'll call you to set up a meeting with the stakeholders when I get back to the office. If you give me their names, I can make contact and get an insight into their interest.'

- To the second one it might be: 'You are absolutely right – this is a fascinating feature and it has many uses that you may be able to utilise outside your working environment. When we have a bit more time I'll show you exactly how it works.'

Cause and effect frame

This frame allows you to explore with your client the effect of what you are doing on the results. You might play around in this frame for some time while you are negotiating prices – for example, so that your prospect can see the impact of their investment on the bottom line.

Possibility and necessity frame

Here again is a frame that is closely linked to metaprogrammes and one that may play a part in influencing your prospect's buying patterns. Does your prospect need the product or are they looking to the future, getting prepared, or maybe it's a 'nice to have'? Knowing this could have a big impact on the timing of your sale.

Agreement frame

This is the frame to use when you are sure you have ironed out all the bumps and your prospect is ready to buy. It simply begins,

'So, are we in agreement that [give a high-level list of what you have agreed, starting with the things you are absolutely sure about] and that we are aiming for a completion date of X?'

You can still use this frame even if you have not reached complete agreement, to summarise the aspects you are clear about and identify those that need some clarification.

Working with frames

Think of frames as a steering device to take you from one block of interaction to another without letting anything within the frame spill out and become uncontrollable. Practise a few at a time until you become adept at working backwards and forward through the frames.

Example

Following a long process of negotiation Paul was visiting his client, having set himself an outcome to gain agreement on the final proposal for the new networked telephone system. He began the meeting by *backtracking* to the original meeting when the client's original needs were discussed. He reminded the client of the alternative solutions (*possibility* frame) that they had considered, and the reasons why they had chosen the one being proposed now. He gained *agreement* that these were still valid before moving forward. He then produced *evidence* that the solution he was about to propose had worked well with other clients and he took time to *contrast* the solution with other less-effective solutions. Throughout the discussion he elegantly answered questions and used the frames to steer the meeting towards his outcome of a signed contract. When he felt they were in *agreement*, Paul openly asked for the sale and received a positive answer.

Successful sales people:

■ use frames to steer their clients through a sales meeting;

■ keep meetings and interactions focused;

■ know how to use frames to help prospects to move forward when they become stuck in their thinking.

10

Selling to groups

In this chapter you will learn how to pull together all the techniques used so far to enable you to engage small and large groups of people. Building rapport with groups requires a special skill set which takes into account a variety of behaviour patterns and decision-making strategies.

Greg's story

Greg is the chief executive of one of the fastest growing companies in the UK. His board decided it was time for some significant expansion and that £60 million was the extent of the borrowing they needed for the next stage of development. Greg had borrowed money from banks before but never on this scale. He harboured a fear of presenting, which he did not want to share with his colleagues on the board, and so he sought help. Learning these techniques not only cured Greg of his fears; he also made a series of presentations to various banks to acquire his finance and then actively began to seek out new opportunities to present his company in new markets, venturing into areas he could only have had nightmares about previously.

Engaging an audience

Probably one of the most excellent but most misused presentation tools of the modern era is PowerPoint. Intended as a 'take me anywhere' tool for giving on-the-spot presentations as well as an illustrator of pertinent points, it has all too often become a crutch upon which presentations are built. As an illustrator or a memory hook, PowerPoint offers some exceptional benefits, but when I see a PowerPoint presentation consisting of lists, tables, figures and bullet points I am immediately aware that the presenter knows a lot about how PowerPoint works but very little about engaging an audience.

How often have you sat through a presentation watching the slides but feeling nothing? How often have you walked away from the presentation thinking 'Thank goodness that's over'? How much did you remember about the presenter and their message? For how long did you sit staring at the slides, trying to read the content as the speaker carried on talking? You only have to go back to the model of communication in Chapter 5 to recall that the mind finds it very difficult to absorb information from a slide at the same time as information from the spoken word. And yet time after time I have sat through presentations where the presenter is in the dark, looking very small, facing up to a huge screen filled with too much information. In such a position it is impossible for the presenter to engage with and build rapport with their audience.

We have learnt enough in the chapters of this book to know that the old adage of 'people buy people' rings true, despite the age of technology and internet buying. People make decisions based on emotional intelligence – it feels like the right thing to do, even if they have gone to great lengths to research and analyse statistics. Yes, it's true that internet buying has eroded this to a certain extent, but you only have to look at the dependence on seller ratings on sites such as eBay to recognise that the emotional aspect of buying still exists even here. If you can't raise the emotional status of your audience, you won't gain a sale.

So what makes a great sales presentation?

In this chapter I am going to give you help making great sales presentations to small and large groups. Here is a summary of the questions you need to ask yourself:

- How well do you know your audience?
- What do you want them to do when they leave your presentation?

- What is your own personal outcome?

- What is the affective message you want to get across about your product or service?

- How are you going to structure your presentation in terms of the sequence?

- How are you going to package your presentation?

- How are you going to truly engage your audience?

- How are you going to make sure you include them all throughout the presentation?

- What personal skills do you need to enhance your credibility and deliver your presentation effectively?

- How can you use PowerPoint as a support and not a crutch, if at all?

Know your audience

Knowing who you are selling to in a group is just as important as if you are selling one to one. Think of your presentation as a gift – you wouldn't buy someone a gift without knowing something about them, and neither should you make a presentation to people you know nothing about. Research your audience in as much detail as you can, finding out about the following:

- Their working environment: is it highly structured or highly creative? Is there a flat management structure or a hierarchical one?

- Their company values: do these square up with what you know about the organisation in terms of its public persona or how you have seen people behaving?

- Their company culture: is it vibrant or stagnating? Are people cautious about each other or open and honest? Is there an air of hope and anticipation or do people seem down-hearted?

- Their competitors: who are they? What do they compete on? Is it price or service or maybe originality?

- The person or people who hold the purse strings: see how much you can find out about the decision-making processes of these people.

- Their main challenges: what is the company currently facing? Are they gaining from the economic climate or losing? What trends are they taking into account in order to stay ahead of the market?

- What these people do in their spare time: are they a cohesive group outside work as well as inside? Do they all frequent the same places or support the same teams? Is there a culture of fast cars or of green issues?

- Anything else you can discover.

It's a gift!

From now on, think of your presentation as a gift. You are going to give your audience something that they truly love and will want to take away and use. In other words, you are going to inspire your audience to take action. You are now going to decide exactly what it is you are going to give them and how you are going to package it to make it easy for them to unwrap and use.

A gift is only valuable if it has some use, so first decide what it is you want your audience to do after listening to your presentation. Do you want them to:

- Sign on the dotted line today?

- Take away some samples and use them for a specific period of time?

- Introduce just one new product line?

■ Get their viewpoint on your next generation of products?

■ Something else?

Whatever it is, write it down succinctly and keep it in mind throughout both the design and the delivery of your present-ation. Keep it simple: never try to introduce too much at once or you may confuse your audience. The bigger the audience, the simpler you will need to keep your presentation.

Your outcome

Decide how you will know whether or not your presentation has been successful. What will you see, hear and feel as a result of a successful presentation? How are you going to measure your success? Even if your audience does not do what you wanted them to do, your presentation may have been successful in other ways. How can you measure this? Maybe raising awareness is a successful result, or maybe getting your audience to reconsider something they were about to become involved in elsewhere is a result in itself and leaves the door open for you to come back at a later stage. Be sure to list as many positive outcomes as you can.

Your affective message

What is the one message you want to get across to your audience about your product or service? Is it to do with the quality, your after-sales service, the uniqueness of the product, its green qualities or something else? What do you want your audience to do as a result of listening to your presentation? How do you want your presentation to affect them?

Structure

You are now ready to put some structure into your presentation. Having a clear structure will not only help your audience to follow your presentation easily, it will also help you to keep the ideas in your head as you make your delivery. It also helps to put your product or service into context. Here are some ways you can consider structuring your presentation.

In time – past, present and future

If you have worked with this client in the past or have been developing your products over a period of time, this is an excellent way to structure your presentation. For example, 'In the past, the xyz product had abc qualities and 123 speeds. In 2005 we added def qualities and increased the speeds to 456. Now in 2010 we have added even more speed to 678 and what I want to present to you today are our exciting plans for the future.'

Big picture to detail

This is an excellent way to show how your product fits into the bigger picture of things. For example, 'Universally, telephone companies are using type two systems to connect people to the internet. This is OK as far as it goes, but increasingly people are asking for more productivity from connections – in fact they are looking for double and treble the speeds. We all know that this isn't going to happen overnight, so we at the Forward Communication Company have come up with an interim solution that is going to greatly benefit your company.'

Concepts, principles and process

Most products or services can fit into a presentation structured in this way. The introduction to your presentation will refer to the concept behind your product or service – another way of thinking about a concept is to refer to it as an idea. For example, 'The idea of product splodge is that it gives you greater flexibility to tie your shoe laces faster. The principles behind this are that thin laces and smooth tips allow for more dexterity in the fingers, so here's how they would work [process].'

Here is another example: 'The idea behind our training programmes is to greatly increase personal effectiveness in the workplace. The principles behind this include greater trainer-to-delegate ratios. We do this through a process of speed-learning techniques, constant facilitation and attention to personal outcomes.'

Example

Richard needed to 'sell' the idea that his company could contribute to saving the planet by reducing waste, recycling products and paying attention to the packaging of its own products. He structured his presentation by first introducing the concept of green practices, highlighting the effect that poor practices were having on the planet currently. He appealed to the emotions of his audience with some soul-stirring pictures. He then moved on to the principles behind the concept, which included reducing waste, recycling and even fighting back against the use of excessive packaging in supermarkets. He left his audience with a process for them to get involved in, which made them feel that they could make a real contribution.

Talking to the whole audience

It is important when talking to a group of people that you include them all. There are a number of ways you can do this. Let's take a look at some in detail.

Engaging your audience

As people arrive for a presentation there is generally a settling down period while they mentally move from their previous activity into your presentation. You can help people to do this quickly and to concentrate their minds by using a number of simple techniques.

Yes sets – getting people on side

This technique is used to get people on your side from the outset. It works on the basis that if you can get people to unconsciously agree with you three times, the chances are they are ready to begin to follow you. For this to work, the statements you make have to be absolutely irrefutable – in NLP we call them universal truths. Here is an example: 'Here we are on a sunny Wednesday afternoon [irrefutable truth 1] in the Continental Room of the Isis Hotel [irrefutable truth 2] ready to explore the use of xyz product [irrefutable truth 3].' There is nothing here that the audience can disagree with and unconsciously they are already preparing to say yes to you.

I'd like to take a moment here to answer a question that I am often asked when introducing such simple techniques. People often say, 'Surely, if this is a common presentation skills technique then people will know what I am doing and will maybe resist it?' The answer here is simple. Think back to the communication model in Chapter 5 – invariably the audience's five to nine pieces of information processing limit is being consumed with the business of arriving at the presentation and casting off any thoughts they have brought with them. They won't be consciously thinking about the techniques you are using – it will be as much as they can do to actually listen to the content of what you are saying. By using these techniques, you are building rapport directly with the unconscious minds of your audience.

Introductory all-inclusive statements – making everyone welcome

Getting people on your side from the outset is going to help you immensely in keeping people engaged and keeping them with you throughout your presentation. An all-inclusive statement lets them know they are in the right place and welcome, whatever their level of experience. Here are some examples:

- *Yes set as above.* This is the third meeting we have held here on this subject – some of you I know have attended all three sessions and others of you are attending for the first time. Whichever it is for you, you are very welcome and I know you are all going to benefit greatly, as well as have a contribution to make either during or after the presentation.

- *Yes set as above.* I know you have differing levels of interest in the products I am going to show you today – some of you will be looking at operating the new systems, others will be looking at the benefits from a user's viewpoint. Whichever it is, I am sure you are all going to have a valuable contribution to make in the next 50 minutes.

Positioning

In order to move your audience to a decision, you need to appeal to them on an emotional level. This will happen through you as a person, not through your slide presentation, which is there only to support some of your points. You need, therefore, to position yourself so that you can speak to and make direct eye contact with your audience. This is not possible if you rely on your slide presentation – your audience will not make an emotional connection with slides, but they will with you. While presenting, make sure you scan the room and make eye contact with as many people as is feasible. Later in this chapter you will learn how to use stage anchors to illustrate and emphasise your points, but for now remember that you are speaking to a group of people and not to a slide presentation.

Taking account of information processing channels

In a group of people you need to make sure that you accommodate the three basic information processing channels – visual, auditory and kinaesthetic. You can do this in a number of ways.

Stories

You can appeal to all three channels by creating a story around your products or services to demonstrate their effectiveness. People with a visual preference will create a movie or a series of pictures in their heads; those with a preference for auditory processing will listen carefully and inwardly digest; and those who process kinaesthetically will explore their feelings around what you are saying. Facts, figures and statistics should be used sparingly, and only to raise the emotional level – for example, 'Did you know that 95 per cent of all computer users only use 15 per cent of a computer's total capacity? It's the same with the human mind.'

I have heard stories used very effectively to explain some very complex products. Here are a few examples:

- The flow of water to describe how money leaks from an organisation.

- A tennis ball passed among the attendees to explain how a complex computer system serves a number of different users.

- The lights in the room where the presentation was being held to explain the complexities of insurance.

- A personal story about how the presenter had been injured in an industrial accident to demonstrate the need for health and safety products.

- Sports analogies to golf, football, tennis and running to illustrate achieving goals.

- A fidgety child who was told she could not concentrate on anything at school, but who went on to be an internationally known choreographer, to demonstrate that not all learning is academic.

The beauty of the story is that it elegantly paces and leads people from something with which they are familiar to whatever it is you want them to buy. Get creative and get passionate about the stories you can tell to demonstrate your products and services. Stories can be personal, third party or made up – the only golden rule is that they demonstrate simply and effectively the message you want to get across.

Stories also have the added advantage of being memorable. People won't remember the facts and figures of your present-ation but they will remember a well-put-together story and the message behind it.

Other ways to appeal to visual, auditory and kinaesthetic processing channels

You can appeal to the different processing channels of your audience in other ways too. The very fact that you are speaking will appeal to those with an auditory preference – make sure you vary your voice tone and emphasise strategic words. Use positive language and cut out extraneous words. Try saying these sentences out loud, emphasising the words in italic:

- This company *will* be setting new goals and targets in the coming months.

- This company will be setting *new* goals and targets in the coming months.

- *This* company will be setting new goals and targets in the coming months.
- This company will be setting new goals and targets in the *coming months*.

See how simple it is to change the meaning of what you want to say just by changing the emphasis on each word.

Remember that people who prefer to use their auditory and kinaesthetic channels often find those who use the visual channel difficult to follow because they speak so fast. Remember to slow down so that everyone in the room can process and absorb information at their own pace.

People who prefer to use their kinaesthetic or feeling channels will be checking their feelings while you are speaking. Decisions will be made on whether or not their 'gut feels right'. They may also play with something while you are speaking – a pen, a piece of paper, their tie, jewellery, hair, or anything that helps them to concentrate.

As a presenter, it is important not to misinterpret body movements. A lot of myths have been written about body posturing, which, if we are to believe them, would put us on the back foot most of the time. For instance, a person sitting with their arms folded is more than likely comfortable in this position rather than defensive. Tapping a pen could just be someone with a kinaesthetic preference satisfying their need to make contact with something. Staring out of the window could simply be someone with a visual preference creating images of what you are saying in order to make sense of your presentation. Tapping feet is often an indication that someone is not used to sitting still for very long and needs to release some energy.

If you interpret any of these behaviours as disinterest then your sales presentation will suffer, because you have taken on a negative belief that may not be true. Stay positive and curious.

Using metaprogrammes to engage and include

When speaking to groups it is important that you cover the extremes of some of the more common metaprogrammes, otherwise unconsciously people will feel excluded. Sometimes your audience may be made up of people who fit a particular profile. For example, an audience of bankers may be prone towards procedural, thinking type behaviour. An audience of advertisers may be more options and towards focused than an audience of insurance agents, and so on. Here are some examples of how you can take account of both extremes of each of the more significant patterns.

Towards/away from

'Some of you, I know, are very excited about the prospect of introducing this line of products – others are anxious not to let go of the benefits of the existing line. Let me reassure you that this new line includes all the benefits of the existing line as well as introducing some new ones that I am sure you are going to enjoy.'

This statement both appeals to those who want to move into new and better things and reassures those who do not want to move away from what is already working well for them. If you feel there is a tension in your audience between old and new, you may use something like this as an all-inclusive statement at the start of your presentation.

Options/procedures

Most audiences include people who like a clear structure around what is happening as well as those who are prepared to play with different options. Both will have a tendency to resist the opposite, so you need to accommodate them both. One way to do this is to introduce the structure around your presentation and then suggest that there will be an opportunity to explore ideas and other options and to ask questions within this structure.

Through time/in time

Accommodating these patterns from a personal viewpoint is simple. Arrive early, remain calm if people keep you waiting and allow time for your presentation/meeting to overrun in your own diary. Again, don't fall into the trap of interpreting lateness as disinterest or disrespect – it isn't. Once the late arrive you will have their full attention, while those who arrived on time need to be reassured that they will get to their next activity on time.

Checking timescales for these people is important, so at the beginning of your presentation make it clear what those timescales are – finish time, time for questions, time for coffee and whatever else is important.

Sameness/difference

This pattern can be easily absorbed into your story. You are taking people from what they know into new and different territory. For example, 'It's like eating clean snow, only softer and smoother' or 'It's like playing a video game in a working environment'.

Internal reference/external reference

Remember that this is about decision making. Internally referenced people will want to make up their own minds while externally referenced people will want some external evidence. Again, appealing to both is a straightforward process. For example, 'Some of you will know instinctively that this is the right course of action, and for those of you who would like more information I have the data here for you to take away with you.'

Global/detail

Great orators know the importance of keeping speeches at a high level. You only have to read the inauguration speeches of people like Nelson Mandela and Barack Obama to realise this. To go into detail is to separate different factions of the audience as well as to upset those who do not have a need for detail. However, it is important to satisfy those who do have a need for detail and one way to do this is to provide printed information for people to take away with them. Telling people this at the beginning of your presentation will effectively allow those who need the detail to relax, knowing that they will get all they need at the end. Do not be tempted to provide the printed packs up front – you will find people reading them rather than listening to the presentation.

Pacing and leading using stage anchors

Example

Stan knew the power of stage anchors. When presenting to groups he would make a mental note of where he wanted to be at different stages of his presentation. For example, he would move to one side of his presentation area to input information and then to the other when he was inviting discussion and questions. When he was looking for a decision, he would walk forward from the middle of the area and make eye contact with the key decision maker. His audience would learn very quickly what was expected of them as he moved about the space, changing the tone and pace of his voice for even greater impact.

We are all anchored into states in some way or another. Any number of triggers can set off a state of apathy, frustration, anger, melancholy, happiness, relaxation, decision making, patience, impatience, feeling sick, feeling light-hearted, feeling good or feeling bad. Sometimes we are not even aware of the trigger, we simply experience the state. Sometimes we are aware of the trigger. For example:

- Whenever I see that person, I become frustrated because ...
- Whenever I hear that song, I feel sad because ...
- Whenever I smell disinfectant, I feel sick because ...
- Whenever I smell flowers, I feel good because ...

In Stan's case he learnt to anchor people's states to where he was standing and to ask for the sale from the middle of the room. You can use this concept in your presentations to create different states in people. For example, if you are going into story-telling mode you can stand at one side of the present-ation area and then return to the centre when you are ready to continue. You could use the other side for when you are inviting questions. This way, your audience will unconsciously pick up the signals that you are ready for something and that they need to be ready too.

PowerPoint

If you are going to use PowerPoint, then follow these golden rules:

- Use it to provide a visual representation of your product or service in action. Make sure this is a picture, cartoon drawing or diagram – but keep it simple and limit the writing.
- Use it for emotional impact – for example, your product being used in third world countries, or to create cleaner working environments.
- Give your audience time to digest the slide – stay quiet while they are looking at it.

- Switch the slide off when you have finished with this particular point, otherwise your audience will continue to look at it instead of listening to you.

- Never put complicated charts, statistics and figures on to a slide. This confuses the mind as your audience struggles to look at the slide and listen to your explanation at the same time.

- Never bullet-point your presentation on a slide. If you talk and ask your audience to read at the same time, you are asking them to use their auditory processing for two things at the same time. Try listening to the sports commentators on TV while reading the information being transmitted across the bottom of the screen – not easy, is it? Furthermore, your audience will know that you are simply using this as a memory aid. If you do not know your subject without this kind of aid, then quite frankly you should not be doing the presentation. If you want to give your audience an overview of the presentation, find a creative way of doing this, using pictures they will remember – talk briefly around each picture, which will explain the structure you have chosen, and then move into your presentation.

Answering questions

Make it clear to your audience how you would like to deal with questions. If you are happy to take them as you go along, say so. If you would prefer to answer them all at the end, then say this and make sure you leave plenty of time.

The secret of answering questions is not to get defensive but to be absolutely clear as to the intention behind the question. It is perfectly acceptable for you to ask for this before answering. For example, 'That's an excellent question – before I answer, I am curious to know what prompted it?'

It is also acceptable to deflect a question if you think that the questioner is trying to be controversial in any way: 'Can I just ask – does anyone else share this viewpoint?' or 'Is this a question that is concerning anyone else?'

If the question is about detail then it is important to validate it, but if you answer it you are going to be sidetracked: 'That's an excellent question and is answered in detail in the information pack I am going to give you at the end of my presentation' or 'I'd really like to discuss that with you – can we meet up later?'

If you honestly don't know the answer to a question then it is better to say so and promise to get back to the questioner later.

The important thing to remember is to validate the question so that you show respect for the questioner and only answer it if:

■ it is relevant to the presentation;

■ you are clear about the intention behind the question.

Getting yourself into a sales presentation state

Once you have prepared your presentation, it is now time to prepare yourself. Decide what an excellent state for making sales presentations is and anchor this state before you start. You may decide that a good state would include being focused, confident, clear, curious and relaxed. Whatever the contents of a good presenting state are for you, you need to access this state, anchor it and maintain it throughout the presentation. Revisit Chapter 6 for the process for anchoring resourceful states.

Staying positive

Finally, I once knew an excellent salesman who lived by the mantra, 'Marry yourself to the cause, divorce yourself from the result.' By this he meant that he always put 110 per cent effort into the sales process but did not allow himself to get despondent if the result did not go his way. He knew there was a market for his products and his job was to find the people who did want to buy, not ponder over the ones who did not.

Successful sales people:

- know and research their audience;
- know how to engage an audience;
- know what they want from their audience;
- structure their presentations;
- keep presentations simple;
- underuse rather than overuse slides;
- remain confident, calm and composed;
- refrain from being judgemental.

11

The NLP sales process

Much has been written about sales processes. In this chapter I will present an overview of the NLP approach to sales, which aims at keeping the sales process simple and memorable.

The four legs of NLP

The four legs of NLP provide an excellent foundation upon which to build a sales process. A successful sales process will ensure that these four legs are in place at every stage. Just like a table, if you remove one of the legs then the whole process becomes unstable.

- **Leg 1: Have a well-formed outcome**. A sales process without a well-formed outcome at every stage is like a ship without a navigation system. A well-formed outcome will keep you on track and ensure that you reach the point you are aiming for, elegantly and efficiently.

- **Leg 2: Have the sensory acuity to know when you are achieving your outcome**. Sensory acuity enables you to assess situations more accurately – when your prospects are ready to buy; when they need to assimilate information; when they have an unasked or unanswered question; when they are feeling excited, uncomfortable, doubtful or anxious. Sensory acuity will enable you to pick up the all-important buying signals or to allow your client more time.

- **Leg 3: Have the flexibility to change course if necessary**. If you practise all the techniques and awareness skills described in this book, you will develop a high degree of flexibility in your behaviour so that when your sensory acuity tells you something else is needed you will be able to change tack and reach your outcome by an alternative route. An inflexible sales person is unlikely to transcend the ranks of the mediocre.

- **Leg 4: Take action.** All the learning, skills and techniques in the world are useless unless you are prepared to take action. Keep control of the process and make sure you keep all the stakeholders in the loop at every stage.

Leg 1: Have a well-formed outcome

As a professional sales person you will have agreed your targets over a set period of time. Your well-formed outcome may go something like: 'By the end of the third quarter we will have increased our sales revenue by 20 per cent compared with the same period last year, with an increase in profit margin of 5 per cent.'

Remember to check the well-formed outcome criteria:

- Is my outcome positively stated?
- Do I have the internal and external resources?
- Am I in control? Is this an outcome I can buy into?
- If I achieve it, what impact is this going to have on me, my team, my customers, my family?
- When I have achieved it, what will I see, hear and feel that will tell me that I have been successful?
- When will I have achieved it by?

If the answers to these questions are all positive, then you have a well-formed outcome and can begin to put together a strategy for achieving it.

Once you have developed your strategy, which will include how you are going to maintain existing levels of business while exploring new areas, keep your efforts on track by developing well-formed outcomes that satisfy the criteria given above for each stage.

Finding new business

Your outcome here may be to develop a new geographical area, or a new market or even to get behind a new product with your existing clients, or maybe a combination of all three. Once you have established your strategy, clarify your outcome for each strand. For example, your outcome for developing a new geographical area might be: 'To find five new customers in the East Midlands region with a total value of £xxxxx by the end of the first quarter.'

You may then decide to design a strategy that includes the following steps:

- Research potential companies on the internet, through local contacts and existing customers.
- Research possible local cultural and economic influences.
- Discover the names of the major decision makers in each company.
- Find out who they currently buy from.
- Find out the values they hold.
- Estimate the potential for your product with this prospect.
- Identify what is it about your products that is most likely to appeal.
- Call the companies for an exploratory conversation.

Your well-formed outcome for your initial telephone call may be something like: 'To introduce myself and find out who the budget holder for xyz products is, so that by the end of the week I have a comprehensive list of qualified potential contacts.'

Continue to build in well-formed outcomes throughout the process. This way, you will not only keep control of the sales process, but you will also find yourself hitting targets elegantly and efficiently.

Legs 2 and 3: Have the sensory acuity to know when you are successful and the flexibility to change your approach

Your sensory acuity will help you, whether you are using the telephone, communicating by e-mail or making a sales presentation.

Using the telephone in the sales process

The telephone provides an excellent opportunity to practise your NLP skills and gain information that is valuable in developing sales relationships. Without the use of the visual channel, you are dependent upon listening for the cues that will enable you to assess your prospect's needs and to pace and lead them to a mutually beneficial outcome. Listen for the pitch, tone and speed of the voice, for the linguistic metaphors and for tell-tale signs of meta-programmes in action. Use your questioning skills to gain clarity and your Miltonian language patterns to pace and lead elegantly.

Skilled sales people learn to listen more than they speak on the telephone. There is nothing worse than a sales person speaking at a hundred miles an hour, ramming their point home on the telephone. Prospects like to be listened to, so finding the right opening and showing your prospect that you care about their issues by listening and responding accordingly is key to success in the sales process.

Have a well-formed outcome for your telephone call and make sure your prospect is clear about the next action. Keep your promise. If you say you are going to call on Wednesday at 3.30 pm, then make sure you do. If you agree to get a proposal to your prospect by next week, make sure you do.

On completion of your call, keep detailed notes of what you have discussed. If social or personal details are discussed, include these in your notes so that you can refer to them when you are next in touch. Remember, this is a relationship and relationships are built on rapport. You will also find this useful in deciding your next step – for example, you may record that the prospect appears to have a procedural pattern and a preference for visual processing. Your next step, therefore, may be to produce a visual flow chart to show the sequence of events that may occur if they were to take on one of your products.

Using e-mail in the sales process

The general rule about e-mail is that it should be used to exchange information only – times, dates, venues, product specifications, meeting summaries, proposals containing no surprises, i.e. the finer points that have already been agreed. You can still gain a lot of information about people from the way they write e-mails and build rapport by matching their style in your response. For example, someone with a value around detail will probably send you lengthy e-mails. If you reply with a curt 'Yes, that's fine' you may inadvertently trample on their values. You need to make sure that you pay attention to and acknowledge the detail in your response. Conversely, if you are asked for just the timing of an event in an e-mail and you reply with a full-blown sales pitch, then your prospect is equally likely to think you do not understand their needs.

Example

Alison received an enquiry from the director of a recruitment company who had been receiving her e-mail newsletters for some time but with whom she had had no previous communication. It was sent via his smartphone and read: 'When is your next personal effectiveness programme and how much?'

Alison responded with: 'February 3–6 £xxx plus VAT. Would you like me to reserve you a place?' Back came the response: 'Yes please.'

Cover all bases in your sales presentation

Make sure your presentation accommodates visual, auditory and kinaesthetic processing. Take in samples, brochures, supporting documentary evidence of the quality of your products and a selection of product/service testimonials.

Mentally rehearse your presentation. Visualise the situation: see, hear and feel yourself speaking, listening and answering questions. Check the tone and pace of your voice – does it sound congruent with what you are saying? Do you need to slow down or speed up?

Dress to match the culture of the organisation – arriving suited and booted in an arty, advertising location will turn your prospect off from the outset.

Profile your client

Keeping a record of your client's profile can significantly enhance your results. An example of a profile you may want to use is overleaf, or, of course, you can build your own.

The example here is a very simple profile – in the early days of practising you may find it useful to put more detail into the profile. For example, you can list the indicators of visual, auditory and kinaesthetic processing in the left-hand column. You could include all the metaprogrammes in the left-hand metaprogrammes box so that you know which ones to look for. You may also find it useful to list your own strong ones initially to make sure that you adjust your behaviour appropriately.

After some practice, and as your ability to recognise patterns becomes more natural, you will not need to record profiles in this way: you will remember them, just as you are able to remember a person's face or tone of voice.

		Notes to self
Client name	Joe Cato	
Organisation	Abacus Bricks	
Times visited	2	
Times spoken on telephone	6	
What is important to this client (values)? **What are their business drivers?** **What are their priorities?**		
Approx. % time spent:		Remember brochures and to draw diagrams of solutions
▪ **Visualising**	50%	
▪ **Listening**	20%	
▪ **Feeling**	30%	Take samples
Words and phrases used by client:		VK combination pattern
▪ **Visual**	I see, take a look, draw me a diagram	Uses look and feel more
▪ **Auditory**		
▪ **Kinaesthetic**	It's beginning to feel right	
Voice calibration:		Remember to up my tempo and pitch to match
▪ **Soft or loud**	Fast and clipped with a high pitch	
▪ **Fast or slow**		
▪ **High pitched or low pitched**		
▪ **Clipped or lyrical**		

Body language: ◾ **Laid back** ◾ **Precise and considered** ◾ **Leaning forward**	Laid back, staring out of the window a lot of the time	Give him time to visualise solutions
Strong metaprogrammes	Global External reference Options Towards	Take testimonials Ask him what other people think Help him narrow down choices to take him forward
Metaphors (e.g. turning up the heat, laying down the stakes, facing the demons, scoring goals)	It's like spinning plates Walking through treacle	How else could he deal with the plates? What would the treacle become if things were working well?
Focus of interest: ◾ **Things** ◾ **Activities** ◾ **Information** ◾ **People** ◾ **Location**	When we first met he noticed my new watch and talked about cars	

Leg 4: Take action

Every stage of the sales process requires action. Setting and keeping to well-formed outcomes will guide the type of action you will need to take at each stage. Make sure that everything you do is in the interest of achieving your sale. It is easy to become involved in 'busy time' – time that is filled with activity but is not necessarily the type of activity that is going to result in a sale.

Building great relationships is not only crucial to the sales process, it can also be a great time saver. I once calculated the time spent by one of my coaching clients in such activities as procrastination, frustration with other people and getting cross when things did not go her way. Tasks that should have taken hours or even minutes were dragging into days and sometimes months because she lacked the co-operation of those around her – all because she had not bothered to build relationships properly. Apply this to your selling career and you can measure in hundreds of pounds the time that could potentially be wasted in this way.

Closing a sale or opening a relationship?

I never have liked the expression 'closing a sale'. This is not to say I underestimate the importance of achieving a signature on a contract and delivering the goods or services, because I don't. It's just that the expression suggests finality and agreeing a sale for me represents the beginning of a relationship – looking beyond the current agreement and paving the way for the next one. Sales are about developing long-term relationships – a sale is a milestone in the relationship. Remembering this can help to keep you focused on the importance of meeting your prospect's needs.

Example

At Quadrant 1 we once turned down a big piece of work with a high street bank. They asked us to 'sheep dip' their IT managers through a programme of management training before a certain date, which coincided with the personal target achievement of the human resources team responsible. After asking a few questions it transpired that many of these managers did not want to be managers and that the training was merely a tick-box exercise so that the human resources team could achieve its targets. To have accepted the work would have contravened our values of quality and results. Some time later we met a member of the human resources team at another company where she had taken up a new role. She told us that the exercise had fallen well short of the desired results, with no real benefit and being a waste of their budget. She respected our integrity for turning down the work. We are now a preferred supplier for the building society she currently works for.

Opening a relationship is a structured process within which you can exercise flexibility of behaviour to facilitate a win/win outcome for yourself, your company and your client. This process is limited only by your creativity and your flexibility to make a positive impact. Your initial sales outcome with a new client represents the beginning of a relationship, which, if handled elegantly and with integrity, will flourish for many years.

Successful sales people:

- utilise the four legs of NLP to structure their sales process;
- believe that a new sale is the opening up of a long-term business relationship;
- are flexible, persevere and stay focused.

Enjoy your selling – and I wish you every success with your career in sales!

Index

Page numbers in *italics* denotes a figure

Also from Pat Hutchinson

David Molden & Pat Hutchinson

brilliant

NLP

What the most
successful people
know, do and say

9780273732556

2nd Edition

Make positive changes with the
powerful tools and techniques of NLP.
Transform your life right now.

Prentice
Hall
BUSINESS

Make a change for the better. Together with our authors we share a commitment to bring you the brightest ideas and best ways to manage your life, work and wealth.

9780273718093

9780273724902

9780273734161

9780273726463

9780273734611

9780273731276

www.pearson-books.com